INTER-
ACTIVE
DESIGN

© 2012 ROCKPORT PUBLISHERS

First published in the United States of America in 2012 by
Rockport Publishers, a member of
Quayside Publishing Group
100 Cummings Center
Suite 406-L
Beverly, Massachusetts 01915-6101
Telephone: (978) 282-9590
Fax: (978) 283-2742
www.rockpub.com
Visit RockPaperInk.com to share your opinions, creations, and passion for design.

10 9 8 7 6 5 4 3 2 1

ISBN: 978-1-59253-780-8

Digital edition published in 2012
eISBN: 978-1-61058-637-5

Library of Congress Cataloging-in-Publication Data
Pratt, Andy, 1977-Interactive design : an introduction to the theory and application of
user-centered design / Andy Pratt & Jason Nunes.
         p. cm.
ISBN 978-1-59253-780-8
1. User interfaces (Computer systems) 2. Interactive multimedia. 3. System design.
4. Industrial design. 5. Graphic arts. I. Nunes, Jason. II. Title.
QA76.9.U83P73 2012
005.4'37--dc23
                                                          2012007628

Design:
Andy Pratt and Samantha Katz

Printed in China

Rockport Publishers
100 Cummings Center, Suite 406L
Beverly, MA 01915

rockpub.com • rockpaperink.com

An Introduction to the Theory and
Application of User-Centered Design

INTER-
ACTIVE

ANDY PRATT & JASON NUNES

DESIGN

CONTENTS

Introduction **p.6**

CHAPTER (1) What Is User-Centered Design and Why Do We Need It? **p.12**

(2) Collaborating with Your Team and Your Client **p.24**

(3) Goals, Users, and Success Criteria **p.34**

(4) Getting to Know Your Users **p.52**

(5) Know Your Competitors **p.74**

(6) Content Is King **p.84**

(7) Designing for the Right Device **p.96**

(8) Guide, Motivate, and Engage the User **p.114**

(9) Building Sitemaps, Wireframes, and Prototypes **p.124**

(10) Branding the Experience **p.146**

(11) What Can You Learn from Usability Testing? **p.166**

(12) If You Build It, They Won't Always Come — Marketing the Experience **p.184**

(13) Watch, Learn, and Adapt **p.194**

(14) Looking into the Future **p.208**

Resources **p.220**
Contributors **p.222**
About the Authors **p.224**
Acknowledgments **p.224**

INTRODUCTION

This book is intended to be an introduction to interactive design in all forms from the web to mobile, from architecture to service design—to give examples of techniques and strategies great designers employ when they want to make experiences for people—that engage people, communicate with them, and encourage them to respond and to interact.

It is now more important than ever for all designers to learn the ins and outs of interactive design—namely, designing for screen-based experiences. Screens are all around us, not just on our computers. Screens incorporate our televisions, cell phones, tablets, e-readers, car dashboards, ATMs, grocery check-out lanes, appliances, and so on. Even if your design career is primarily focused on print, motion, or industrial design, there is a good chance that what you design—your product or experience—will extend into the interactive digital world in some form. What you design will incorporate, or be shown on, a screen.

It is also worth mentioning that some of the best interactive designers come from traditional design backgrounds—print, motion graphics, even creative writing.

That said, this book is intended for design students, traditional designers, and anyone interested in gaining a basic understanding of interactive design and user-centered design (UCD) practices. This is not a step-by-step how-to guide—partially because we believe that there is no perfect process that applies to all design. Rather, we will highlight successful interactive projects that have incorporated user-centered practices. We will explore what those practices were and why they resulted in more successful design.

In its simplest form, UCD means designing for individuals. It means putting the human, or user, at the center of the design process. We believe that following a user-centered process, with a focus on understanding and meeting the needs of real people, leads to more successful design, more useful products, and more fun! After all, human beings are social animals.

Of course, all design projects are different. There are many variables that have to be taken into account—including strategies, budget, schedule, who's paying the bills. We have over thirty years of experience designing for the web, mobile devices, kiosks, set-top boxes, tablets, and other devices. We have designed tools, applications, games, and interactive experiences for consuming (and creating) content of all forms—from photos to video and beyond. Our many experiences, both successes and failures, have led us to believe that designing for real people, understanding who they are, and what they want, where they live, and where they work, and ultimately meeting their unmet needs, leads to better design, more successful products, and more satisfaction as designers.

We hope that this book will expose young designers to a new way of thinking about and approaching design that will ultimately lead to more satisfying design.

— Andy Pratt and Jason Nunes

100
USER EXPERIENCE BACKGROUNDS

Our online survey for user-experience (UX) professionals asked three questions: What is the professional background that led to your UX position? Where do you live? What is your current job title?

In the interest of full disclosure, this survey hardly met the guidelines required by the scientific method. "Professional background," for example, is a little vague. But as we expected, the results indicated a varied range of backgrounds for this profession. As colleges and universities continue to develop programs to meet the needs of interactive design, this landscape may well shift, becoming something that more people engage in at an earlier age.

We found the variety of job titles included in the survey interesting. Many were expected, such as director of user experience, UX design lead, and information architect. However, titles such as front-end developer, design director, and computer engineer were a little less obvious, suggesting perhaps that a certain degree of UX proficiency is now expected in other interactive professions. Our favorite title: hackstar.

As digital design continues to expand, new professions will grow out of its changing needs. For example, a survey about content strategists or social media managers may well have revealed a similar diversity of backgrounds and titles. The field is changing all the time. You may look back one day and be surprised at how your job as a designer has evolved.

PROFESSIONAL BACKGROUND OF **PARTICIPANTS**

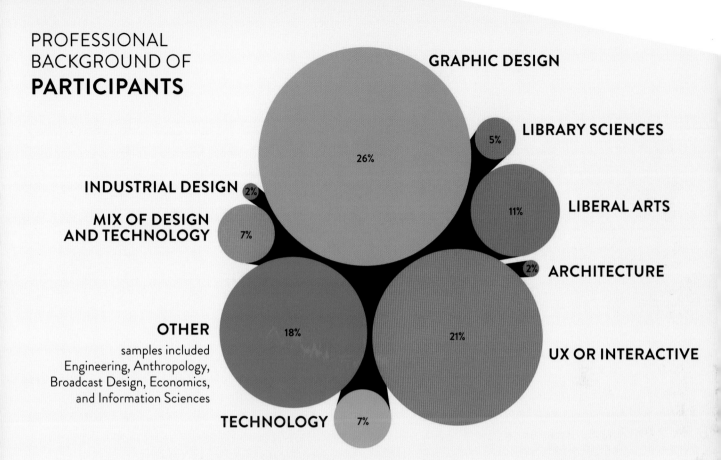

GRAPHIC DESIGN

26%

LIBRARY SCIENCES
5%

INDUSTRIAL DESIGN
2%

LIBERAL ARTS
11%

MIX OF DESIGN AND TECHNOLOGY
7%

ARCHITECTURE
2%

OTHER
samples included
Engineering, Anthropology,
Broadcast Design, Economics,
and Information Sciences

18%

21%
UX OR INTERACTIVE

TECHNOLOGY
7%

LOCATIONS OF **PARTICIPANTS**

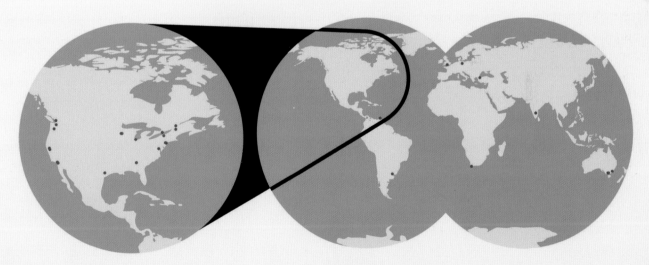

UNITED STATES		CANADA	VENEZUELA	TURKEY	INDIA
Portland	St. Paul	Toronto	Porlamar	Istanbul	Hyderabad
Seattle	Chicago	Montreal	BRAZIL	UNITED	AUSTRALIA
San Francisco	Atlanta	Vancouver	Buenos Aires	KINGDOM	Sydney
Los Angeles	Austin		GERMANY	London	Geelong
Mountain View	Burlington		Berlin	SOUTH	Melbourne
Pasadena	Rochester			AFRICA	
Santa Monica	New York			Cape Town	
Minneapolis	Brooklyn				
	Washington, DC				

Illustration by William Ranwell

"19th-century defined by the century by the culture of the will be defined interface."

culture was novel, 20th cinema, the 21st century by the

Lev Manovich, referenced by
Aaron Koblin in his TED2011 talk, March 2011

User-centered design (UCD) is a design philosophy that puts the user of a product, application, or experience, at the center of the design process. In UCD, a designer strives for a detailed understanding of the needs, wants, and limitations of the people who will use the end product and then makes design choices that incorporate this understanding.

UCD requires that designers not only analyze and foresee how users engage with a product, but they also test their designs in the real world with actual users. Testing is an essential component of UCD, because it is often very difficult for designers to intuitively understand how users will perceive, understand, and use their designs.

ArmCoach

Dinis Meier and Samuel Bauer,
Zurich University of the Arts, Zurich, Switzerland

After a stroke, patients are immediately forced to deal with their new physical limitations. These often include partial or complete immobilization of one side of the body. The rehabilitation process is slow, exhausting, and may cause people to neglect their therapy. This only delays their recovery, often leading to depression and further frustration.

Continued on page 14.

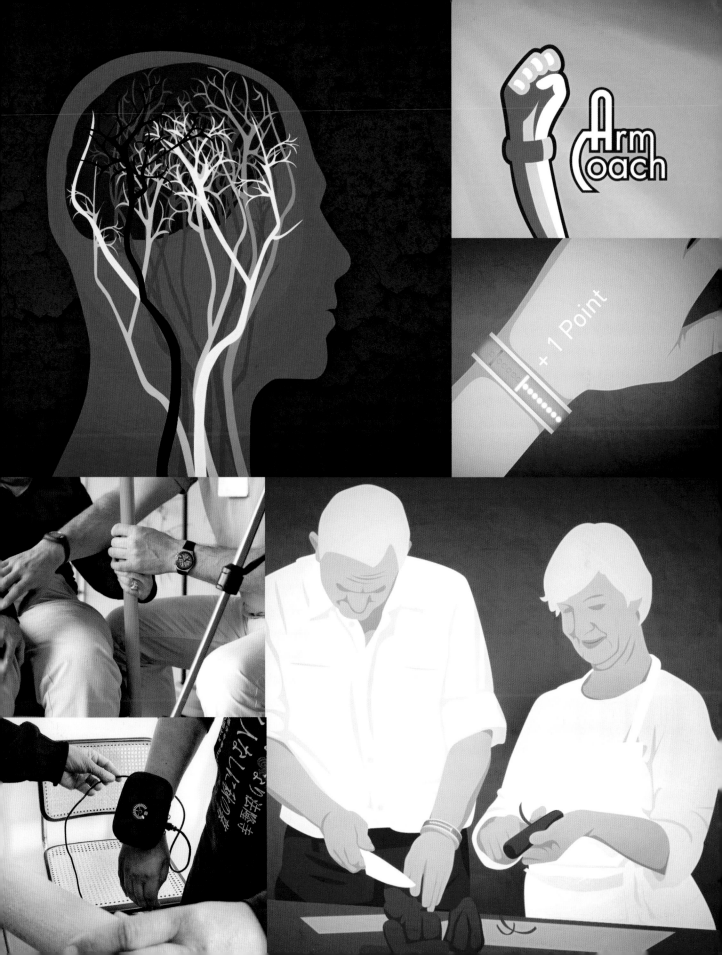

Continued from page 12.

ArmCoach is a product concept that uses motivation to change this dynamic. Patients wear a bracelet that reminds them to move their impaired arm on a daily basis. As they do so, small LED bars light up.

The more bars that light, the more points the patient earns. This information feeds into an online web app, so users can track long-term progress and receive practical tips on arm exercises. The product empowers patients, as they feel that they are more in control of their recovery.

Prior to design, the design team used field observations and interviews to learn more about the patients, their relationships with their therapists, and the challenges they face together.

The team created several prototypes to test the product in real situations. These prototypes provided important qualitative feedback, leading to more refined models. Overall, the response from users was extremely promising.

Products designed with a user-centered approach can have a meaningful impact on a user's life. The conceptual design of ArmCoach has been well received, and several companies are interested in developing it further.

Learn more: Google ArmCoach

ArmCoach Case Study |
Dinis Meier and Samuel Bauer,
Zurich, Switzerland

A brief history of user-centered design

In the 1940s, human factors engineering and ergonomics were design processes that attempted to create physical objects such as airplane cockpits that took into account human physiology—the shape of the human body and the way it works.

In the 1960s, with the birth of cognitive psychology, the idea of "ergonomic fit"—a design fitting the human body—evolved into "cognitive fit"—a design taking into account and "fitting" the limits of our senses, deductive ability, and memory. This new concept of cognitive ergonomics was quickly incorporated into the burgeoning field of human computer interactions (HCI), which examined how human beings would interact with and use these radically powerful, new designed objects—computers.

In the 1970s, ethnographic research techniques such as shadowing and contextual interviews were incorporated into the burgeoning philosophy of UCD, giving designers powerful new tools to learn about their users.

Today, UCD is a pervasive design philosophy that is most often applied to interaction design (IxD), which is the process of designing interactive digital products from websites to video games. But UCD is also used to design many other things—from architecture and silverware to cell phones and street signs.

UCD is a powerful set of tools that any designer can use to create better designs.

UCD
and IxD

Putting the users in the center of the interaction design process, and taking into account their wants and needs, increases the potential that the designer will create interactive products that are easier to learn and use and are more successful and fun. However, even though UCD is widely applied in interactive design, no IxD project is ever purely user centered. Nothing is designed where the only considerations taken into account are users' needs, goals, and wants.

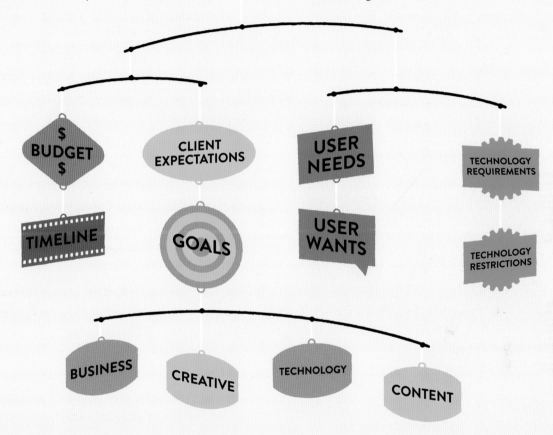

Many other factors must be taken into account when designing an experience. These factors can include the business goals of the client, the limitations of the technology used to realize the design, the timeline for delivery of the finished product, and the budget.

Balancing these different factors and incorporating user needs and wants can be challenging. But if your goal is to design elements that are actually built and used, these factors must be taken into account. A finished project is more successful than an unfinished one.

Whatever the process, the best digital products meet the needs and wants of real people. A designer who understands what they are communicating through a design, how that design will be realized, and who that design is intended for, will have a much better chance of designing a successful product or service.

Why is UCD so useful?

We live in an increasingly overwhelming world. The people we design for are inundated by information and noise. Walk down the street and you'll see billboards and street signs, you'll hear music and traffic, or you may get a text message or cell phone call.

We use data and information to help us navigate the world, to be entertained, and to help us make decisions. Electronic devices feed us that data.

Well-designed information is visible to us when we need or want it. Well-designed devices take into account the factors of the environment in which we use them. Well-designed objects take into account our bodies, offering clues as to how they will be used by their affordance or shape.

Understanding who we design for, what they want and need, and the environment in which they will use our designs, is not only a good way to guarantee a successful product, but also a safer, saner world. Poor design can be frustrating, preventative, and in extreme cases, deadly.

BAD UCD CAN BE DEADLY

Excerpted from "The Secret Language of Signs" by Julia Turner at www.slate.com. First published March 1, 2010.

"Thirty-three members of the Bluffton University baseball team boarded a bus at their campus in Bluffton, Ohio. It was early evening, and the college students had a long night ahead of them—an 18-hour ride, punctuated only by bathroom breaks, fuel stops, and a planned breakfast at McDonald's. But their destination was enticing: Sarasota, Fla., which promised sunshine and the first game of their season.

"After an uneventful overnight drive, the bus stopped in Adairsville, Ga., to pick up a fresh driver, then headed south on I-75, eventually entering the H-occupancy vehicle (HOV) lane. As the bus rolled closer to Atlanta, it neared the turn-off for Northside Drive, the first of several left-hand HOV exits that dot that stretch of highway. The driver, Jerome Niemeyer, should have kept right where the road split, continuing toward Florida in the HOV through-lane. Instead, he took the left-hand exit ramp at highway speed, apparently mistaking it for a regular lane. At the ramp's end, he drove through a stop sign and four lanes of traffic before careening into a retaining wall and flipping onto the highway 19 feet below.

"The accident killed seven people—five of the Bluffton players, the bus driver, and his wife, Jean, who was along to keep him company. When the National Transportation Safety Board investigated, it blamed the crash in part on Georgia's failure to install adequate signs."

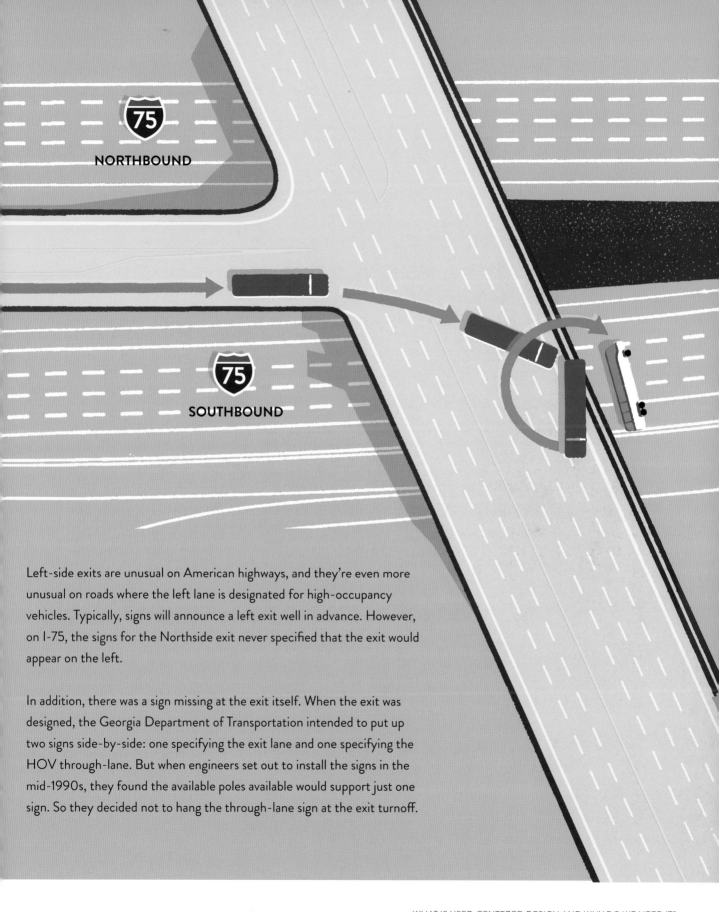

Left-side exits are unusual on American highways, and they're even more unusual on roads where the left lane is designated for high-occupancy vehicles. Typically, signs will announce a left exit well in advance. However, on I-75, the signs for the Northside exit never specified that the exit would appear on the left.

In addition, there was a sign missing at the exit itself. When the exit was designed, the Georgia Department of Transportation intended to put up two signs side-by-side: one specifying the exit lane and one specifying the HOV through-lane. But when engineers set out to install the signs in the mid-1990s, they found the available poles available would support just one sign. So they decided not to hang the through-lane sign at the exit turnoff.

"Your users are redesigning your real time. Users co-designers imagine all the actually use what

continuously
user interface in
become your
because you can't
ways someone will
you create."

Dana Chisnell, principal researcher
at UsabilityWorks

Principle Six

Principle Six (P6) is an online movement to create a better food system. It allows consumers to discuss and rate the products in their local food co-ops.

Here's how it works: As consumers shop at these markets, they are encouraged to join the P6 site and nominate their favorite products to be inducted into the P6 Hall of Fame. In order to qualify for P6 status, products must meet two of the following three criteria: They must be grown or made by a small farmer or producer, locally grown or produced, or sold by a nonprofit business or co-op. Users may nominate any product they think may meet the criteria, giving motivation for other members on the site to vote and review these products. This gives the farmers and co-op organizations valuable feedback and publicity. Ratings by P6 staff, co-op stores, and member nominations also influence which products are being considered for the prestigious P6 Hall of Fame.

The success of the site is completely dependant on user participation. Sevnthsin designed the site to foster community participation, create a forum for discussion, and ultimately reward the farmers and makers for producing the best products.

Principle Six homepage.

The Story of Your Food

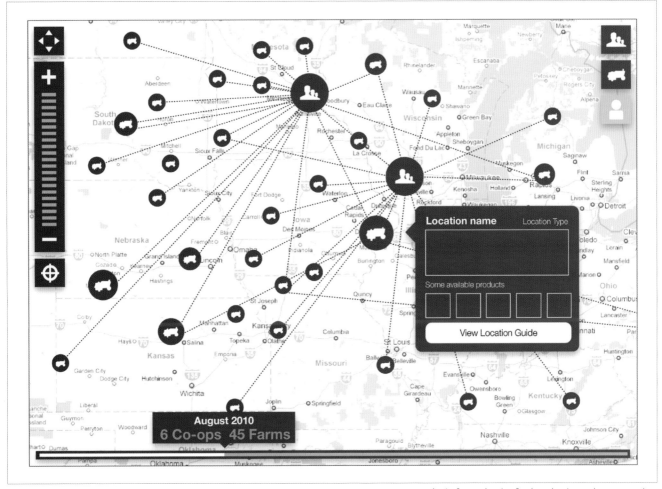

A wireframe showing food production and transportation.

It became clear to Sevnthsin midway through the project that they were designing for the wrong user, in this case, someone unversed in the merits of whole, natural foods. Original concepts of the site were geared toward education on food systems. One example: wireframes focused on visualizing the complex journey processed or nonlocal food takes before it gets to the plate. Features and functionality like this, although interesting, placed a lot of emphasis on education. The client decided to focus on users that already supported the local whole food movement, and this changed the way Sevnthsin looked at the goals and functionality of the site.

Principle Six Website | p6.coop
Sevnthsin, Minneapolis, MN

WHAT ARE AFFORDANCES?

Donald Norman, cofounder of the Nielson Norman Group, describes affordances as, "the perceived and actual properties of a thing, primarily those fundamental properties that determine just how a thing could possibly be used." Think of them as the visual clues that help you understand how to use an object.

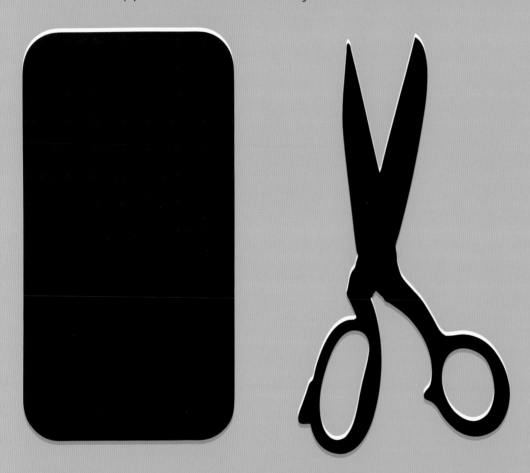

Compare the silhouettes of an iPhone to a pair of scissors. These scissors have several visual clues that may help a user understand how to use it. There are clearly two large openings, probably large enough for fingers. It also has a fulcrum in the center, which seems to suggest the device will open and close. The scissors afford cutting. The iPhone, on the other hand, has no visual clues. When the phone is on, artificial clues are needed. Three-dimensional-looking buttons help afford clicking. The lack of affordances also required another important clue to help users know what to do after the iPhone is turned on. Tell them, "slide to unlock."

Recommended reading: The Design of Everyday Things *by Donald A. Norman. Basic Books, 2002.*

MENTAL AND CONCEPTUAL MODELS

In her book, *100 Things Every Designer Needs to Know About People*, Susan M. Weinschenk describes a mental model "as the representation that a person has in his or her mind about the object he is interacting with. A conceptual model is the actual model that is given to the person through the design and interface of the actual product."

This is an important difference to understand. People create a mental model about an object or experience in an attempt to predict how the object will behave. Part of the design process involves understanding the user's mental model when he or she sees an interface or experience. Sometimes the design team may want to change their conceptual model to match a user's mental model in order to ensure the experience will work the way the user expects it to.

However, sometimes designers want to develop a conceptual model that creates an entirely new mental model or alters an old one. User testing with this approach often results in frustration for the participants. They don't have a clear mental model, so they don't know what to expect. Repetition, clear messaging, and training are great ways to create a new mental model for them.

It is also important to understand that mental models are learned over time, and build on top of one another. Imagine trying to define an online social network to people in the 1950s. They would have no idea what you are talking about. In order to do so, they would need to have a mental model of a personal computer. Then they would need a mental model of the Internet, followed by a mental model of a browser.

However, if you ask people today for their mental model of a social network, they will probably think of something like Facebook. Friend feeds, statuses, liking and sharing are all interface elements that people have come to expect. If you had asked the same question years ago, the mental model may have looked more like MySpace or Friendster. What will social networking look like in twenty years? We don't have the mental models yet to answer that question.

Due to their limited life experience, younger people have fewer mental models than adults. This means every mental model they do have is significant. Have you ever seen a toddler with an iPhone or iPad? Swiping through the interface soon becomes second nature to them. As a result, they develop a specific mental model about how other objects will behave. And these expectations extend to other non-touch-based screens, like laptops, ATMs, and TVs. They tend to think that everything functions like a touchscreen. Toddlers may also apply this mental model to objects other than screens. Put an advertisement for an iPad or iPhone in front of them and they may think it is a broken device, not an ad printed on paper.

Recommended reading: 100 Things Every Designer Needs to Know About People *by Susan Weinschenk. New Riders, 2011.*

It's not my fault I don't understand how to use your product

CHAPTER 2

Collaborating with Your Team and Your Client

Before you meet your client and users and start designing something innovative and desirable, it's a good idea to get to know your fellow team members.

Design has never been a solitary pursuit. Architects work with teams of engineers, drafters, and other specialists, as well as builders and contractors to realize their designs. Print designers collaborate with content specialists, illustrators, photographers, and printers to bring their designs to life. Interactive design is no different. User experience designers partner with a variety of different team members, who bring different expertise to the proverbial design table. These teammates and design partners bring skills and perspectives that are essential to building a website, game, application, or mobile app.

A UX designer will work closely with the following:

- Technical architects who are charged with designing the systems and code that will realize the design
- Visual designers who are tasked with incorporating the brand personality into the design
- Content strategists who are responsible for the content that the application will convey to customers
- Project managers who are responsible for making sure the design project is completed on time and budget.

They may also partner with many others, including product strategists, subject matter experts, and business strategists.

These six departments represent the foundational core needed to create a great interactive experience or product. Depending on your digital product, you may have other departments as part of your team. For example, if you have ad units or sponsorship opportunities, you may have a dedicated sales team. If your product deals with education, you may have curriculum specialists. Your team will also look different if you are part of an in-house product team as opposed to a client services team. Smaller teams often have team members fulfilling the responsibilities of multiple departments. For example, a user experience lead may also be the content strategist, or a web designer may also be the information architect.

Note: This list is not intended to be comprehensive. Each department has a wide variety of roles that are not included here.

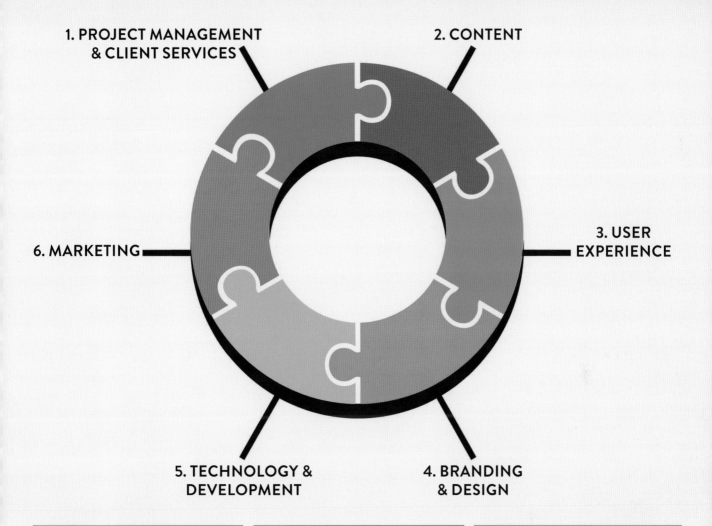

1. PROJECT MANAGEMENT & CLIENT SERVICES

2. CONTENT

3. USER EXPERIENCE

6. MARKETING

5. TECHNOLOGY & DEVELOPMENT

4. BRANDING & DESIGN

---

1. PROJECT MANAGEMENT & CLIENT SERVICES

A great product is possible only when things stay on track.

SAMPLE ROLES:

Account Executive

Project Manager

Producer

2. CONTENT

A great product starts with relevant, quality content.

SAMPLE ROLES:

Content Strategist

Managing Editor

Content Migration Specialist

3. USER EXPERIENCE

A great product is desirable, usable, and enjoyable

SAMPLE ROLES:

Director of User Experience

User Experience Designer

Interaction Designer

---

4. BRANDING & DESIGN

A great product is on-brand and is visually appealing to the demographic

SAMPLE ROLES:

Creative Director

Art Director

Designer

5. TECHNOLOGY & DEVELOPMENT

A great product is responsive and the technology feels invisable

SAMPLE ROLES:

Technology Lead

Developer

SEO Specialist

6. MARKETING

A great product is great only if users know about it.

SAMPLE ROLES:

Digital Marketing Strategist

Social Media Manager

Search Marketing Specialist

DESIGNING AND BUILDING TOGETHER

by Anders Ramsay, user experience designer and product strategist

With software products becoming evermore complex, spending hours and hours creating static Photoshop comps before starting to build the real product is becoming less cost effective. Sure, your design may look sweet, but will the wheels come off when it is made interactive?

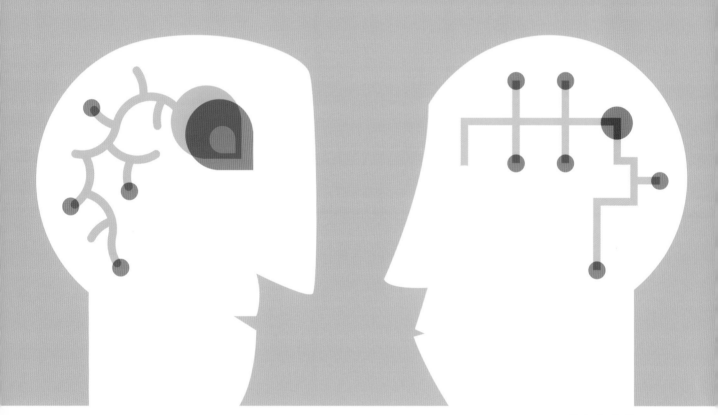

Illustration by Samantha Katz

A great solution to this is cross-functional pairing, whereby a designer and a developer sketch, design, and build the final product together. It's like two players running up a field, continually passing a ball back and forth, with it at first more in the hands of the designer, but shifting to the hands of the developer as you get closer to the end zone. If you've never tried it, this might seem a bit scary, but when you discover how quickly you are able to go from idea to working software, you may not want to go back to working individually.

Try this when adding a new feature to an existing product that has some established design patterns. After doing some basic research—which you are encouraged to also do as a pair—start by sketching individually for five minutes and then share your ideas. This will get you warmed up and create a good foundation for your collaborative work.

In front of a whiteboard, sketch out an overall user flow and high-level design of major screens. One factor that makes this type of session powerful is that you are looking at the same ideas with different eyes. A developer might offer an alternative to an idea you propose that you didn't even know was technically possible. Or, you might improve the usability of an idea proposed by a developer with just a few minor tweaks.

It also can be helpful if one person has a background in UX. However, by virtue of your different design perspectives, you are effectively creating an instant usability feedback loop. If neither of you have a background in UX, consider getting occasional feedback from a UX specialist.

When you have consensus on a design direction, shift your work to start building a skeleton version of your design. A developer can help determine when it makes sense to start building and stop sketching.

Working side-by-side, the designer might continue sketching in more detail or creating the look and feel while the developer is coding. Because you are working physically next to one another, you can get quick, informal feedback on one another's work.

In just a few hours, you can go from an idea on a whiteboard to a functioning web page. While it may be rough around the edges, it is still something far closer to the actual design solution than a static design comp, allowing you to get highly reliable feedback from clients, users, and other team members.

Recommended reading: Designing with Agile *by Anders Ramsay. Rosenfeld Media, 2012.*

Collaboration is critical

Interactive projects are complicated. To build them, multiple computer languages may be required. They may have to integrate with existing client systems such as content management systems or ad management solutions. They may have to work on multiple platforms—from laptops to mobile devices. Clients may have very strict brand guidelines that must be followed. The content that your project will provide to users must be understood. What format is it in? How often is new content created?

Each member on an interactive design team brings a unique perspective to a project—perspectives informed by their expertise and experience. A technical architect may suggest a different way to design some aspect of a project based on how easy it is to build. A visual designer may recommend ideas for how to make a design more fun, or more concise, based on their understanding of your client's brand. A content strategist may suggest a design that showcases the best verbiage. A time-crunched project manager may propose using an existing off-the-shelf component rather than custom design some part of the project.

In order to juggle the various complicated aspects of interactive design, it is essential to collaborate. Interactive teams must feel comfortable communicating with each other and making suggestions, even if those suggestions fall outside of their areas of expertise. Sometimes the best suggestions about how to meet user needs come from team members who are more concerned with technology or making sure that a content production schedule is achievable.

'You'd be surprised what clients will tell you if you just ask. A lack of feedback is rarely a sign that you're on the right track."

Courtney Deakyne, director of marketing/client strategy, Sevnthsin

Don't Forget to Collaborate with Your Client

Collaborating with your team will ensure that you are able to understand all the different complex perspectives of an interactive project. Collaborating with your client will guarantee that you design and build a successful product of which everyone can be proud.

Clients bring their own expertise to the table. They understand their customers. They also understand integrating existing technical systems, working with different client teams, the intricacies of their brand identities, and design visions for the project. They can be powerful and useful partners.

By working with them and presenting different options and recommendations, and ultimately making decisions together, you will meet the wants and needs of your users and the goals of your clients. You will design and build something useful and desirable within the allocated schedule and budget.

Bon Iver website design.

Bon Iver

When Sevnthsin redesigned the Bon Iver website, they knew it would be challenging. The site launch had to coincide with the album release, which was quickly approaching.

With only a few weeks to complete the project, Sevnthsin's usual development process had to be truncated. This didn't mean skipping steps or cutting corners. It meant defining expectations quickly, locking down features and functionality, and imposing strict client feedback and approval deadlines. It also meant keeping to one round of wireframes and designs—an arrangement that requires a lot of communication and trust on both sides.

Sevnthsin gives full credit to the client for being so flexible and decisive. It was integral to the project's success.

Bon Iver Website | boniver.org
Sevnthsin, Minneapolis, MN

YMCA Twin Cities

While working on the redesign for the website for the local YMCA Twin Cities, the team at Clockwork found a great way to collaborate with their client. The process began with a typical brainstorming exercise: They asked their client to pick words that they associated with their brand. The YMCA came up with: accepting, hopeful, powerful, and authentic. Words like these help provide a general sense of the experience, but their ambiguity makes it challenging when translating them into pixels on a screen.

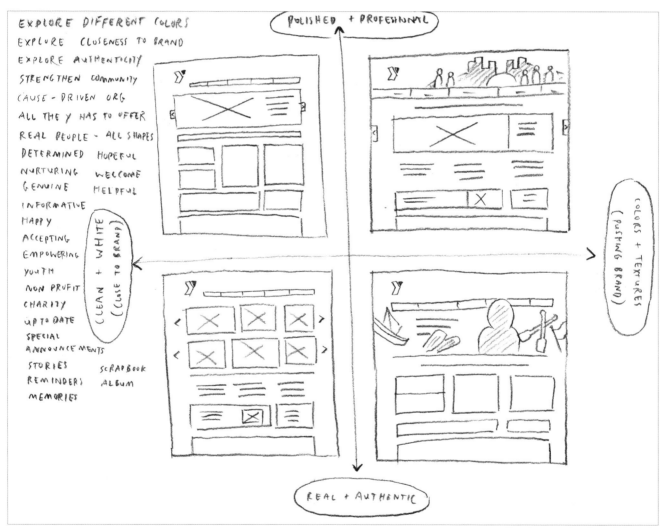

Sketches were placed on a 2x2 matrix.

Clockwork was able to turn these abstract descriptors into quick sketches to show to their clients. By visualizing the experience early on in the process, the client could quickly see the possibilities for the site.

YMCA sketch.

This sketch is not too far from the final design.

This also allowed the client to eliminate ideas they felt were not on target. One of the sketches displayed a rendering of the Minneapolis skyline in the background. The client knew, based on user research, that this approach would alienate residents in the outer boroughs if the site felt too focused on the more urban centers. Not further exploring this option saved valuable time and money.

YMCA Twin Cities Website | ymcatwincities.org
Clockwork Active Media Systems, Minneapolis, MN

Goals, Users, and Success Criteria

Design is about making choices—deciding to use one font over another, what information to display, or what feature has prominence on a page. Design choices can be as much about what elements to include as they are about how to display the information and its functionality.

But how do we make these choices? Is it just our gut instinct? Is it what we like? Clients hire us partially for our unique perspective, but they expect us to apply that perspective in an informed way. They want us to make choices based on our users and on meeting their specific needs and goals. The work we do for our clients should help them be more successful, make more money, reach more customers, communicate more clearly, and make great customer experiences.

By understanding and prioritizing what both our clients and their customers want, we can make the strongest design choices. Prioritized goals inform choices, mediate arguments, and help determine when a design is successful.

The World Park

Looking to attract a younger, tech-savvy park visitor, The World Park turned New York City's Central Park into an interactive board game. More than 1,500 people played at the first event, setting an important benchmark metric for future events.

The World Park
Agency Magma, New York, NY

Goals

One of the first steps in any design process is to understand what you are building. Kick-off meetings and deep dive sessions with client representatives help a designer understand what his client wants, but often this kind of brain dump can make a designer feel as if his client wants everything.

As a designer, especially in a UCD context, it is your job to help clients articulate their goals for the design. Not only what they hope to create, but why. Do they want to make more money? Get more users? Create more buzz? We call these "wants" business goals.

Business goals can range from the simple—increasing the number of ads seen by customers—to the esoteric—raising awareness of an issue such as ocean stewardship. Often just having a discussion with clients in which they create a list of business goals can lead to greater clarity and a unified perspective.

Pricetag homepage design.

Pricetag

When the custom quoting tool Pricetag was being developed, project goals were quickly identified and prioritized. This allowed team members to quickly get on the same page and focus limited resources on the highest priority goals.

Pricetag Website | Pricetaghq.com
Pricetag, LLC, New York, NY/Quito, Ecuador

We sometimes think of our clients as a single entity, but more often they are groups of individuals who represent different sides or departments, all with slightly different perspectives. Discussing business goals can help them reach consensus and make your job as a designer easier. Once goals have been identified, it is essential to understand which are the most important. Prioritizing business goals can take time and diplomacy, but it is necessary. Often, clients want to prioritize all business goals as "high," not realizing that this will ultimately lead to poor design. Designs that try to meet all goals end up overly complex, confusing, and unsuccessful. Focused design is important. A prioritized set of business goals helps create focus.

One tool we have used successfully with clients is a prioritization pyramid. First, we have our clients write down all their goals on sticky notes. This makes it easy to add, subtract, and reorder the goals. Next, we have them physically place the notes on a pyramid split into three quadrants—high at the top, medium in the middle, and low at the bottom. We encourage them to place 20 percent of the sticky notes on the highest section, 30 percent in the middle, and 50 percent in the lowest. It doesn't always work that way, but just going through the process helps clients make decisions and focus.

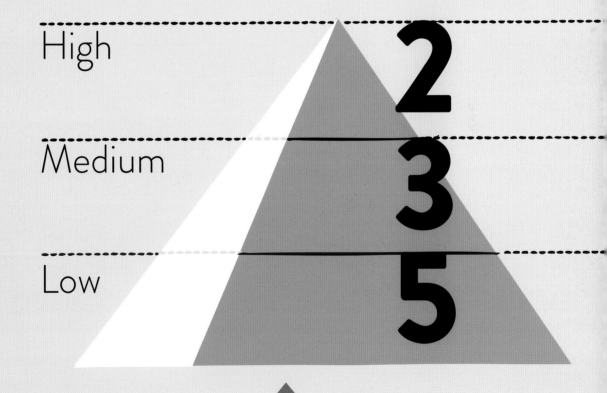

Don't get top heavy!
A pyramid is smallest at the top. If a client identifies ten goals, only two goals should be high priority.

"As our concept phase down, we revisit assumptions to make any

begins to wind
our early goals and
recalibrate and
needed changes."

Julie Beeler,
principal, Second Story

Users

Next, it is important to get your client to talk about users. Who are their customers? Who do they think will end up using what you design? Some clients have lots of specific demographic information about their customers—age ranges, income levels, education, etc—and some will want you to design for everyone.

It is just as important to get your client to define and prioritize their users as it is to get them to list their business goals. You can't design something for everyone. Encourage your clients to talk about the nondemographic information they know about their customers. Who are these people? What tribes do they belong to? What are their interests? What do they do? Often, it's not just a client's customers that are users of a design, but the clients themselves.

At first, this information may come out as an unorganized set of observations, traits, or roles—our customers are tweens, use skateboards, or use Twitter. It's important to write down every trait and stick it to the wall. When they suggest a trait that seems related to one already suggested, group them together. Eventually, an initial user list will emerge based on this grouping of demographic and psychographic (personality, values, attitudes, interests, or lifestyle) information.

Next, it is vital to have your client prioritize this user list in the same way they have prioritized business goals. Who do they see as their primary users? Who is secondary? Who is important to consider, but shouldn't be used to make design decisions? It is also important to understand how these different user types might interact with each other. What will they share? How will they need to communicate? Will they affect each other?

All of this information is a first step to creating a user ecosystem—a prioritized list of user types that illustrates how they interconnect and interact. When you begin your user research, the user ecosystem will be essential in determining on whom to focus.

Who is your primary user?
The simplest way to understand for whom to design is to prioritize your user groups from highest to lowest. This is a great exercise to do with your client. Different stakeholders may have different opinions when identifying their primary user groups.

Etsy product page.

Etsy

Etsy, the popular online market for handcrafted goods, has two primary user groups: buyers and sellers. They each have different experiences that are tailored specifically to them.

Etsy Website | etsy.com
Etsy, Brooklyn, NY

YOU CAN'T DESIGN FOR EVERYONE—AND YOU SHOULDN'T!

I was reminded of this when Jason [Nunes] and I recently went to a client meeting. We were in the elevator when I noticed that the button for the sixth floor was bright plastic orange. This seemed out of place. Although the building was small, every detail was beautiful and considered, and orange was not in the color palette. In a little bit of premeeting small talk, I brought up the oddity of the orange button. "Oh, I wish they would finally fix that button," they remarked. "It is incredibly ugly."

On the way back down, I noticed that the main floor button was also the same cheap-looking orange plastic. I wondered if the buttons were temporary fixes or if something else was going on.

As it turns out, those two buttons were part of a system, one that was not designed for me. The sixth floor of that building is home to an organization for the blind and visually impaired. For those users, the distinct texture and color of the orange buttons are clear and simple navigational devices.

Success criteria

Work with your clients to define success criteria. These are measurable ways to determine if a design has done its job. For example, success criteria could include a 50 percent increase in page views for an existing website, or 30,000 downloads in the first six months for an app.

Success criteria are essentially business goals applied to the user ecosystem represented in some measurable way. So a business goal might be "to make more money." To determine success criteria, it is important to know how a company might achieve this. For example, to increase revenue, a client could display more advertising by increasing the number of visits to their site. But who are the visitors? A client's existing customers could be offered a more engaging experience that would encourage them to view more pages, or new customers could be enticed to check out the site for the first time. Both could meet the business goal. But both require different design solutions.

Parking Wars 2 start screen.

Parking Wars

In the Facebook game Parking Wars 2, users monitor and maintain their street by ticketing their friends' cars when they park illegally, thereby earning virtual cash. Their friends do the same. These actions indicate what users like and where they spend their time within the game. This helps determine what new content and features should be considered to keep them coming back.

Parking Wars 2
Area/Code, New York, NY

The goal of "making more money" applied to the user ecosystem might be translated into the success criteria, "increase visits to the site by new users by 25 percent." It is really important to understand what success looks like to a client. If you have multiple stakeholders, their expectations may not be the same.

The high-priority business goals should have success criteria tied to them. For example, if the goal is to increase buzz, a success criteria might be the number of web searches for your product or site after its launch, or the number of mentions in blogs or on Twitter. If it's difficult to determine how a business goal might be measured—for example, an increase in ocean literacy—work with your client to determine how they would measure this success, and then build a test into the project to see if you've met their expectations.

What does success look like?

Metrics are just data. They help to create a basis for comparison. The success of a project needs to be evaluated over time. And what they are clicking is as important as what they are not. If an area of the experience is not meeting the success criteria, it can be tweaked.

Online sales
Repeat customers
Number of comments
Unique site visitors per day
Individual page impressions
Unique site visitors per month
Number of Twitter followers
Number of shared items
Number of downloads
Time spent on site

"Metrics what users dislike, but tell you dream

can tell you
ike and
they can't
what they
about."

Scott Gursky,
game designer

Features and Functionality

You can work with your client to create a prioritized list of all the features and functionality that will be included in your design. In the simplest terms, functionality is what your design will do, and features are how it will do it. These terms have become somewhat synonymous, and the line between them can get blurry, but it's a good idea to define and differentiate them up front with your client. For example, a function of the website might be offering users a video to watch. A feature would involve how they find it—by browsing through categories or seeing what their friends have watched.

Encourage your clients to list the features and functionality they envision. They may even add new features and functions based on the business goals and user ecosystem you've begun to define. Make sure they understand that just because a feature or function goes on the list, doesn't mean it will automatically be included in the design. As we've already stated, the best designs are focused, which often means judiciously leaving things out of the design.

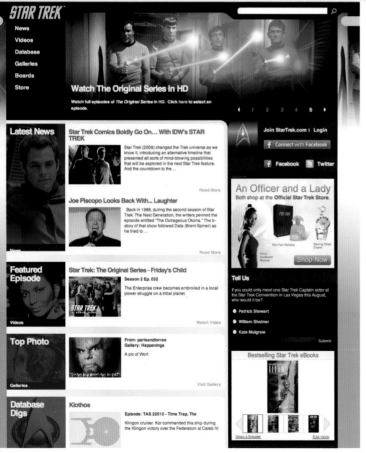

Star Trek home page design.

Star Trek

The new website Startrek.com is aimed at both seasoned and new fans. Surveys and focus groups indicated that neither group was interested in Star Trek–related games, so they were not included in the final design.

All Star Trek fans wanted the ability to watch full episodes. This feature was not available on the older version of the site, but was included in an attempt to bring in new fans. It is always a good idea to align business goals and user needs.

Star Trek Website | Startrek.com
Funny Garbage, New York, NY

Once you have defined the list, you can prioritize it. This can seem daunting for clients who may be uncomfortable prioritizing features and functions because they assume this will mean that the eventual design won't do everything they imagine it to do.

Look at each feature and function and then ask the questions: Does this meet a business goal? Does this serve a user type? Determine how important a specific feature or function is to the business and to the user, average these together, and voila, you've got a prioritized list of features and functionality.

Now you're ready to design, right? Not so fast. First, it's time to meet your users.

Star Trek video player design.

Time to filter and focus.

You and your client will brainstorm a lot of ideas for potential features and functionality, but do they support your client's business goals? Do they support one of the primary user groups? Use your prioritized goals and user needs as a way to help filter the information so you can focus on the features and functionality that matter most.

BADGES

STREAMING VIDEO

RSS

CONTENT MANAGEMENT SYSTEM

MESSAGE BOARDS

POLLS

PHOTO GALLERIES

BLOG

FACEBOOK LOG-IN

USER-GENERATED CONTENT

GAMES

USER COMMENTS

GOOGLE MAP INTEGRATION

ADS

SLIDE SHOWS

TWITTER FEED

USER PROFILES

E-COMMERCE

FACEBOOK FEED

AVATARS

LEADER BOARDS

RATING

FILTER

SUGGESTED FEATURES & FUNCTIONALITY

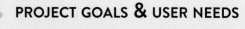

PROJECT GOALS & USER NEEDS

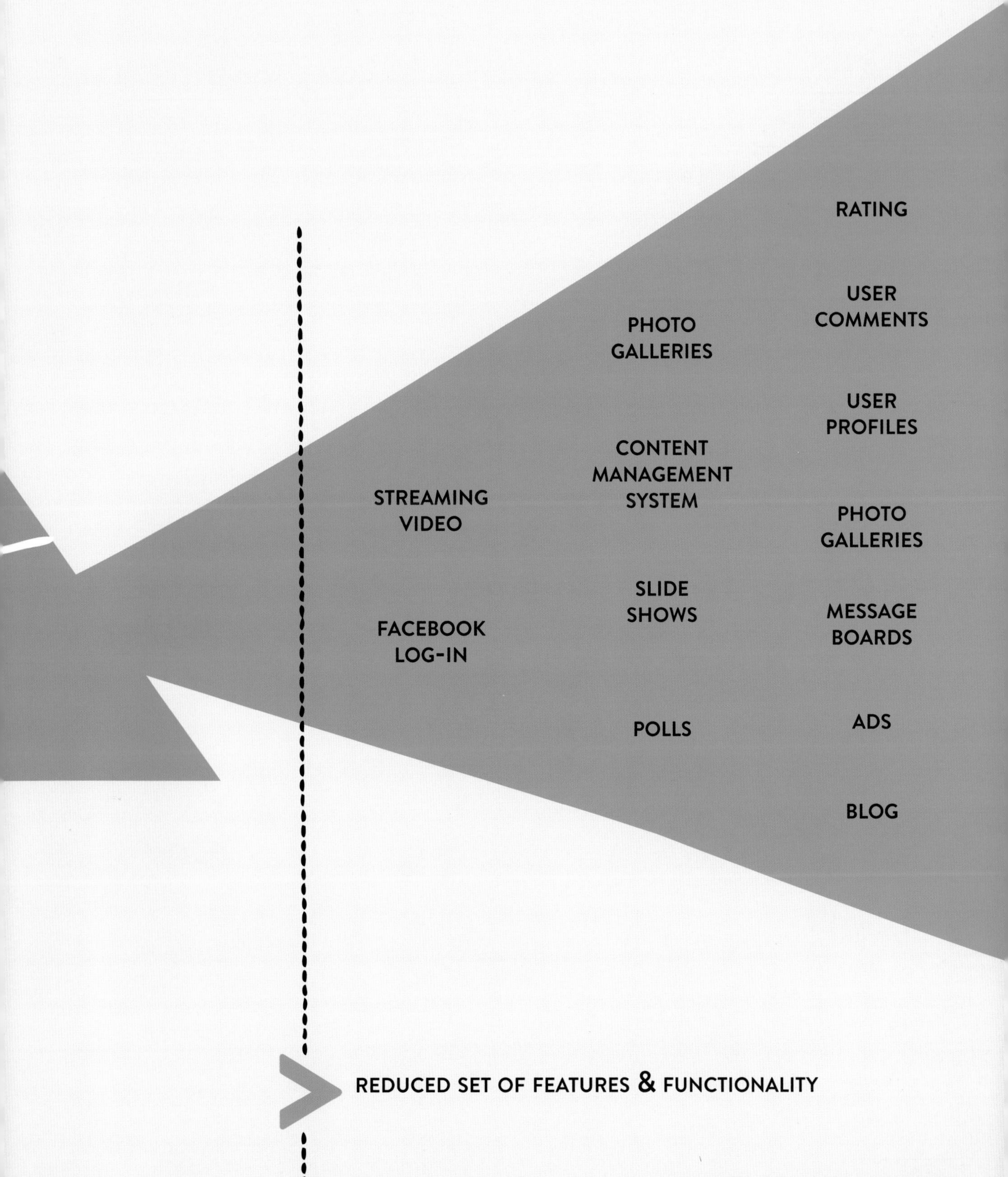

RATING

USER
COMMENTS

PHOTO
GALLERIES

USER
PROFILES

CONTENT
MANAGEMENT
SYSTEM

STREAMING
VIDEO

PHOTO
GALLERIES

SLIDE
SHOWS

FACEBOOK
LOG-IN

MESSAGE
BOARDS

POLLS

ADS

BLOG

REDUCED SET OF FEATURES & FUNCTIONALITY

TRY IT:

USING STICKY NOTES AS A TOOL FOR REQUIREMENTS SESSIONS

As we've already hinted at, your best friend in initial meetings are sticky notes.

It's important to create the impression that nothing is set in stone yet. Not features, functions, users, or business goals. As you progress through design, learn more—about your competition and your users—and begin to make choices. Doing so, the design will become more concrete. But in these initial kickoff meetings, it's important to be open to all the different options and visions.

Start out each exercise—whether you're defining business goals or user types—by being open to everything. Encourage your clients to share all their ideas. And when they do, write them down and stick them on the wall. When you come up with your own ideas, write them down too and stick'em. You will be pleasantly surprised at the kinds of conversations this type of activity can create.

Once you've got a solid list of all the options on the wall, start to group the 'ike' options together. Pull a sticky off the wall, and restick next to one that's similar. It's good to get all your clients involved in this. Put them in groups of two or three, get them on their feet and have them group stickies. Again, this will create more useful conversations as they discuss and debate why some stickies belong with other stickies.

Eventually, you'll create a set of groupings, which should be named. Each grouping is your initial business goal or user type. Write each grouping name on another sticky. And stick it.

Now it's time to prioritize. Draw a pyramid on a whiteboard or large sticky sheet. Explain to your clients the 20/30/50 rule—20 percent of their goals should be high priority, 30 percent medium priority, and 50 percent low priority—and set them loose. Have them work in groups to move the newly defined business goals or user types onto the pyramid. Encourage discussion and debate. You can learn just as much from listening to their internal discussions as you can by the final prioritization of goals or users.

Give it a try. It's not only useful, but it can turn the dullest meeting into something lively and fun.

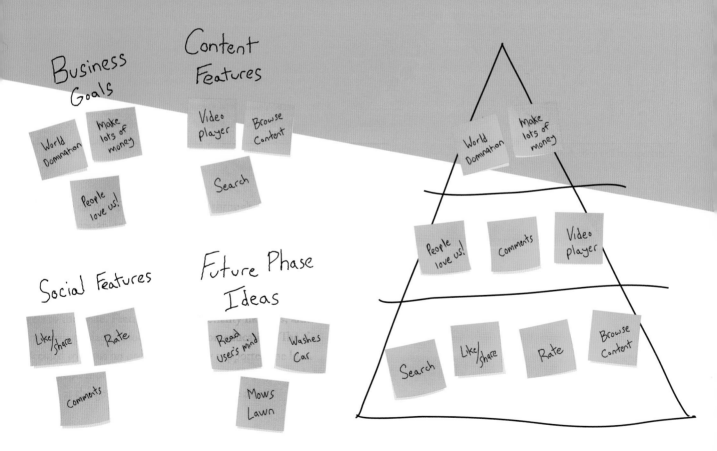

Getting to Know Your Users

It's time to put the user into user-centered design. Once you've met with your client and worked with them to understand their business goals and vision for the design, the next step is to learn as much as you can about who you will be designing for—your users.

The most successful products and projects meet the needs and wants of real people. Those who come from different backgrounds, have different experiences and levels of expertise, and like and want different things. What we design will be used by these different people in specific situations and places. To make great design choices it is important to understand these details.

For example, if you are designing a hand-held ultrasound device, you'll need to know if it will be used by a doctor who has been working a twelve-hour shift in an emergency room. To make good design choices, it is essential to put yourself into the shoes of that doctor. What does her fatigue feel like? How is the room lit? How much time will she have to use the device? What kinds of decisions will she make based on the information she receives from the device? And the doctor isn't the only person to understand and consider. In the case of a medical device, it is important to understand the needs of the other user in the room—the patient.

The things you design will be used by and affect real people.

University of Oregon Ford Alumni Center

The University of Oregon's Ford Alumni Center came to Second Story with an unusual goal. Unlike many university alumni centers, the Ford Alumni Center is equally focused on the future as it is the past. They aimed to create a place that simultaneously honored the history of the student body and attracted the next generation of graduates. To accomplish this goal, the Portland-based interactive firm utilized the architecture of the space to create an interactive experience that is anything but ordinary.

Continued on page 54.

University of Oregon Ford Alumni Center interactive table.

Continued from page 52.

Given the unusual blend of audiences engaging with the Ford Alumni Center, research proved especially crucial in the creative process. Second Story conducted a far-reaching survey of former and current students. They followed this with interviews to determine what makes attending the University of Oregon unique. In so doing, they were able to hone in on "areas of overlap": certain experiences and feelings shared by former and current students alike. This information was the bedrock upon which the entire project was built.

This interactive table combines playfulness with information: it recognizes every individual alumnus of the University.

Interactive media mixes with physical artifacts in these giant panels, each of which commemorates the past, chronicles the present, and imagines the future.

The University of Oregon Ford Alumni Center
Second Story Interactive Studios, Portland, OR

Telling the user's story

So how exactly do you learn about your users? What about them do you need to know? How do you communicate what you learn about them to your clients? And ultimately how do you use that information to make choices?

Once you've worked with your clients to define a set of user personas, and have a basic understanding of for whom you will be designing, there are a variety of ways you can learn more about your users.

The first step is to find real people who are similar to the personas you've defined. UXers often call these people "user representatives."

Clients are a good resource to identify user representatives. They will often have contact information of existing users through their sales and marketing teams. These user representatives are a great resource, but their experience with your client may color their opinions. It is best to try to find different user representatives with different levels of experience with the product you are designing.

Another way to find user representatives is to reach out to family members, coworkers, or friends who are similar to your defined personas, or to go where potential user representatives might be. If you were designing a touchscreen airline kiosk, it's a good idea to watch travelers at an airport check-in gate.

Learning about your users

Once you've identified your user representatives, there are many different techniques you can use to learn about them.

In the case of the airline kiosk, the most effective technique is just to hang back like a fly on the wall and observe them. Are they rushed and frustrated or happy and excited about their trip? Do they want to check themselves in or wait in line to talk to an agent? You will probably find that there are many different types of users—from seasoned business travelers to first-time vacationers. You may decide to create more personas from what you learn.

Other ways to learn about customer representatives include one-on-one interviews, surveys, focus groups, and work shadowing.

When meeting with a customer representative one-on-one, prepare some open-ended questions. Encourage them to tell stories about their lives or work, as well as talking about the product you will be designing. Try to get information about who they are and what they do, and not just their opinions about what you will design.

Surveys are a great way to gather more detailed information from your user representatives. Once you have some understanding of who they are, their environment, and what they want, you may find you still have questions. Write those simple questions and invite user representatives to answer them. We used a survey in the writing of this book to try to understand more about what working UXers did before they became UX designers.

Focus groups are similar to one-on-one interviews. They can help you understand how a group of users views a product or their work environment. But they can also help you get a sense of how your users may interact with each other. Often, it is good to break a focus group into small groups to complete collaborative exercises. You can learn much by listening to how your user representatives talk to each other.

A focus group is a great way to learn about the perceptions, beliefs, and attitudes toward a product, concept, service, or experience in a group setting. A moderator leads the discussion, making sure it stays on track and covers relevant topics, while other moderators observe and hand out materials. We often segment our focus groups based on the different user types rather than mix them all together.

My favorite technique for learning about users is shadowing. Similar to "fly-on-the-wall" observation, shadowing is when you follow a user representative throughout their day, watching what they do, and who they interact with. Asking questions is a big part of shadowing, but the wealth of information you will glean will come from watching. The stories people tell about themselves are often very different from what they do.

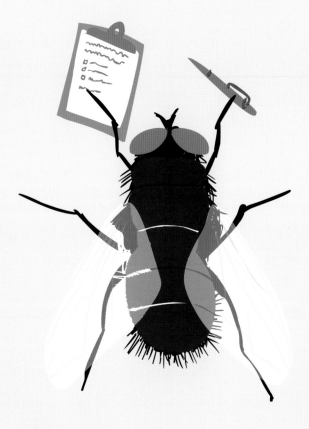

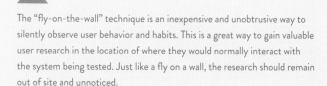

The "fly-on-the-wall" technique is an inexpensive and unobtrusive way to silently observe user behavior and habits. This is a great way to gain valuable user research in the location of where they would normally interact with the system being tested. Just like a fly on a wall, the research should remain out of site and unnoticed.

TIP Surveymonkey.com is a great tool to create online surveys.

Kicker Tea Tumbler prototype.

Tea meets technology

After water, tea is consumed more than any other beverage in the world. Early records indicate tea drinking occurred as far back as tenth century BCE So when the team at Kicker Studio decided to use technology as a way to enhance brewing tea—a time-tested process devoid of technology— they needed to learn a lot about their users in order to convince them to try something different.

Kicker Studio identified four guiding design principles by interviewing tea drinkers, chatting with tea shop owners, and observing baristas at work:

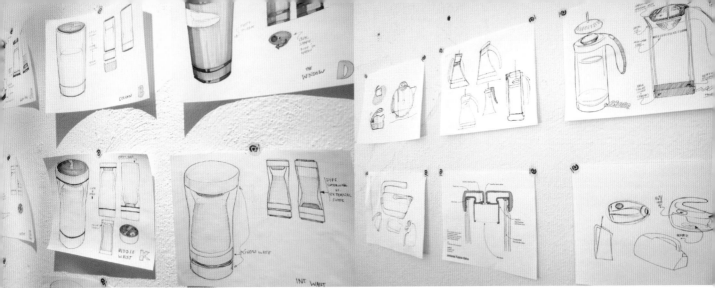

Kicker Tea Tumbler sketches.

1. Respect the Ritual.
No new steps, nothing that feels like a dramatic change.

2. My Tea, My Way.
Allow tea drinkers the flexibility and control to make the tea how they like it. Allow for adjustments on the fly.

3. Not Just Taste.
Tea is about the senses.
Design for sight, smell, and warmth, too.

4. Digital Enhancements, Analog Experience.
The process should feel like something low tech. No screens.

The simple but powerful concept of flipping the teapot over to stop the heating process and start the brewing process allowed for the teapot to be free of clunky interfaces like screens and buttons. Rounds of prototypes and lots of testing ensured that the interaction was clear and intuitive.

The final result was the Kicker Tea Tumbler, an elegant upgrade to an age-old process. As Kicker Studio puts it, "The focus is on the tea, not the technology."

Kicker Tea Tumbler
Kicker Studio, San Francisco, CA

What do you need to know?

What kinds of information do you need to gather about your users? Some of this will depend on what you are designing. If you're designing an airline kiosk, you don't necessarily need to know about their taste in entertainment, but you might if you're designing a mobile gaming interface. We believe that the most successful products are designed for real people. Gather as much information as you need to see your personas as real people.

That said, it is important to understand some basic information about your users, such as age, education, and background. What is their technical competency and familiarity with the technology you are designing? Where will they be using it? What is that environment like? How much time will they take to use it? How often? How much time will pass between each use?

Additionally, it can be useful to know about their tastes and hobbies. What do they do for fun? Video gamers may have a very different set of expectations of an interactive experience than movie goers or marathoners.

It is also important to know about how they interact with the digital landscape. What are all the ways your users access information and connect with other people? An iPhone user has a different set of expectations than someone with a regular cell phone. Do your users communicate on Facebook or through text messages? All this can impact your design choices.

Lastly, it is important to learn any information that is specific to what you're designing. Do your users have a special vocabulary or set of guidelines that they follow that will affect what you design? In the case of the hand-held ultrasound device, it's important to not only understand medical jargon but also emergency room culture.

> **TIP** Set up a focus group on Facebook. The social web can be a great place to informally gather information about your users, especially if you are short on time or money.

Personas

Personas often include a photo, a name, a quote from the persona, a list of descriptors, such as where the person works, their marital status, and their interests, a list of their goals and needs, and a paragraph or two that explains in detail who the persona is, what they want, and what their frustrations are.

Some design companies will print up large pictures of their different personas and hang them on the wall where team members can see them. This acts as a reminder that whenever a decision is made—design, business, or technical—it should take into account the needs and wants of the people for whom the team is designing.

"A good persona[ ]be used throughout[ ]Reference your personas[ ]designs and talk about[ ]presentations. Give life[ ]you'll end up designing a[ ]people they represent."

can—and should—
the life span of a project.
n the wireframes and
them in meetings and
to your personas and
great experience for the

Dan Willig, user-experience
designer, Funny Garbage

User scenarios and stories

The next step is to begin to tell the story of how your persona will use what you are designing—a user scenario. This narrative often takes the form of a story. An average user scenario is one to two paragraphs long. It communicates details of who the persona is, what their specific needs are, and how they will meet those needs using what you design.

The best user scenarios read like great stories. The characters are interesting and sympathetic. Their needs are easy to understand. The barriers to meeting these needs are clear. And, ultimately, they win. They meet their needs through what you and your team will design and build, and their lives are made better.

Communicating what you learned

How do you communicate what you've learned about your users to both your clients and your team members?

It is easier to design for a person you have in mind than to design for a set of data. Demographic data is valuable in finding user representatives, but it doesn't help when you're confronted with design decisions.

The first step in communicating what you've learned is to write a biography of the different users you've identified. Turn the data you've gathered into a biography of what seems like a real person, but is fictional—a persona.

Use cases

User scenarios tell the persona's story at a high level. The next step is to tell the granular, specific stories of how the persona will use what you design to meet the small goals—like registering for an account or browsing for content—that are required to tell their full user scenario.

Use cases are mini stories that explain the steps a user will take to perform an action. Usually several sentences in length or a list, they are written in the present tense and start with a clear goal such as "the user needs to turn on the hand-held ultrasound device"; followed by user interactions, such as "user turns on the device's power"; and responses from the system, such as "the start-up screen is displayed, indicating that the device is powering up."

Use cases are especially useful in determining the details of what you will design. Walking through the story of a user's detailed interactions with each part of a system or application, helps you understand all the different kinds of functionality and information you will need to design in.

Document failure as well as success. Fail cases, sometimes called exception flows, are a special kind of use case that details what happens when the user makes a mistake or the system can't perform the requested action. Fail cases are often ignored during the design process. This can result in additional functionality after an application has been built and can lead to a confusing interface. If you have the time, write your fail cases at the same time you write your use cases.

By understanding your users, including their needs and stories, you can design something that will be useful and valuable. But you're not quite ready to begin designing yet. Now that you understand for whom you are designing, and what their needs are, it's time to learn as much as you can about how they are currently meeting those needs. It's time to understand your competitors.

The Ocean Portal

Funny Garbage was hired by the Smithsonian Institution's National Museum of Natural History to create the Ocean Portal—an interactive online experience aimed at fostering curiosity, awareness, understanding, and stewardship of the world's oceans. Early on in the process, user personas were created for some of the primary audiences.

Reviewing the user personas with the client helped identify that teachers were an important user group to attract, because they will use the portal to introduce ocean literacy to their students. Initially, the Ocean Portal team thought to include detailed lesson plans. But teachers revealed that creating lesson plans was something they wanted to do so they could tailor them to their specific needs.

By providing the raw materials for creating lessons, the Ocean Portal could become an even more valuable resource for teachers. The designers learned that even teachers who weren't teaching classes specifically about the ocean, would use the materials for classes such as mathematics or civics. Testing early assumptions with the teachers shifted the content creation efforts to include activities, as well as lessons. By including a powerful way for teachers to filter materials based on grade, subject, and topic, the For Educators section of the Ocean Portal has become a valuable educational resource.

The Ocean Portal | ocean.si.edu
Funny Garbage, New York, NY

The Ocean Portal homepage design.

Persona 1:
The Teacher

Name:
Jane

Background:
The schedule of a high school science teacher is demanding. In the fifteen years that Jane has been teaching, she's spent many evenings searching for current reference materials to use in her lesson plans.

Needs:
Scientific information and materials can be incorporated into her strictly regimented curriculum.

"It can be difficult to find reputable, up-to-date materials that I can use in my lesson plans for biology class."

Jane's Scenerio

Jane is about to begin teaching a section on human impact on coral reefs. She determines that the life sciences textbook she uses in her course does not have enough detailed information or specific lesson plans and homework on the topic. Mostly because understanding human impact is constantly changing, and her textbook is now five years old.

Jane's first stop is Google: She searches for "coral bleaching" and while unsurprised by the usual suspects—Wikipedia, National Geographic, and NOAA—she is surprised to see a fantastic image of coral polyps in the Google image results from the Smithsonian.

Jane's first stop at The Ocean Portal is the Coral Reefs Ecosystem page with the large image of the polyp highlighted. Jane clicks through a few more images then on a beautiful video of a coral polyp's life cycle. Jane looks at the other Coral Reef content subpages and is delighted to see so much detailed information about coral organized by simple-to-understand topics, like Featured Creatures, Threats and Solutions, and especially Human Connections that even has a link to an article all about coral bleaching. Then Jane notices a link to a prepared lesson plan about coral. "Too good to be true," she thinks. But what the heck, Jane clicks.

Jane's next stop is the Coral Lesson Plan. There is a downloadable PDF presentation that she can project, as well as printable handouts, a classroom activity, links to more resources about coral, and a link to an OPP story about coral (with associated learning objects). "Huh? What's a story?" thinks Jane. She decides to check it out.

The six-chapter-long story is all about the Smithsonian's efforts to rear Elkhorn Coral in captivity. Jane clicks through several of the chapters. The story is compelling and focused enough to keep her students interested.

Jane's User Flow

Jane clicks back to the lesson page, downloads the lesson materials, copies the link to the story, and breathes a sigh of relief.

She clicks over to the Educators' Corner landing page, and is happy to see a variety of additional plans, with a message letting her know that more will be posted monthly. Jane bookmarks the page. Then she notices that she can subscribe to a New Lesson Plans RSS feed to be notified when new lessons are posted. She subscribes, and copies the URL and instant messages it to her fellow science teacher, David.

Jane plans her next class lesson.

```
Start:
Google
Search
  │
  ▼
Coral
Ecosystem
Page
  │
  ▼
Download  ◄──  Views Coral  ◄──►  Coral
Lesson         Ecosystem         Bleaching
Plans          Subpages          Article
                │         │
                ▼         ▼
Educator's              Coral
Corner Page             Lesson
  │                     Page
  ▼                      │
Bookmarks               ▼
Page                  Elkhorn Coral in
  │                   Captivity Story:
  ▼                   Chapter 1
Subscribes              │
to RSS Feed             ▼
  │                   Elkhorn Coral In
  ▼                   Captivity Story:
Shares Link  ──►  Stop  Chapter 2
to Page
```

KEY

- ☐ Page
- ▤ Page Stack
- ◇ Decision
- ▢ Terminator
- ▢ Task / Action
- 🗎 File
- 🗎 File Stack
- → Flow Line

Persona 2:
The Aspiring Oceanographer

Name:
Josh

Background:
As a young boy growing up on the coast, Josh always loved the ocean. Even on the coldest days, he swam along the coast with his goggles on, looking for sea creatures. He is considering a major in marine biology when he heads to college in a couple years.

Needs:
A fun, informative online experience where he can find information about various sea creatures.

"I'm going to do something about the planet!"

Josh's Scenerio

Josh is combing the Internet on one of his regular searches for more information about the environment and the ocean when he gets an e-mail from his younger brother Jonathan about a website. He often sends Josh anything ocean-related he finds when doing homework. Josh follows Jonathan's link to The Ocean Portal's The Ocean and Us page.

Josh already was aware that the ocean is facing many challenges today, but he knew there was a lot more to learn. He sees a link to an article recently published about conservation efforts and their effect on sea life. Along with the article are photographs and links to outside research. Here are the facts he had been searching for!

After reading several articles about conservation efforts and getting some additional information on the ecological risks the ocean faces in the near future, Josh notices that dolphins, his favorite animals, are one of the species in danger. He follows the trail of information and is both dismayed by the dangers he reads about, and enthralled by video clips of dolphins swimming in schools. He makes sure to note many of the connections between the animals he adores and the environmental issues he was reading about earlier, and the site makes those connections really easy to understand.

Wanting to know what more he can do, Josh jumps over to pages about future efforts and how he and others can get involved. He already knew about sustainable seafood, but he learns even more about other ongoing programs, and tips for sustainable lifestyles. On one of the pages, he follows links to one of the Smithsonian's partner institutions and signs a petition to prevent overfishing in the North Atlantic, and puts his name down to volunteer at a conservation education program near his home. He returns to The Ocean Portal to make a donation to the Smithsonian and to add The Ocean and Us page's RSS feed, so he can immediately know about new programs and information when it's posted.

Josh is excited about the possibilities available to him, but knows that in order to really make a difference, more people need to be involved. He wants to see if The Ocean Portal has ways to help him spread the word. First, he downloads some of the more dramatic news to share with interested parties, then he emails some of the articles to his friends and colleagues on the marine biology website message boards. He also goes to the articles and photos he found most alarming and tags them with keywords he thinks potential conservationists might search for.

After leaving The Ocean Portal, Josh logs on to Facebook, becomes a fan of the Ocean Portal, and posts about the site on his profile and a few friends' walls, and gets back to spreading the word about saving the ocean with the new resources he's found.

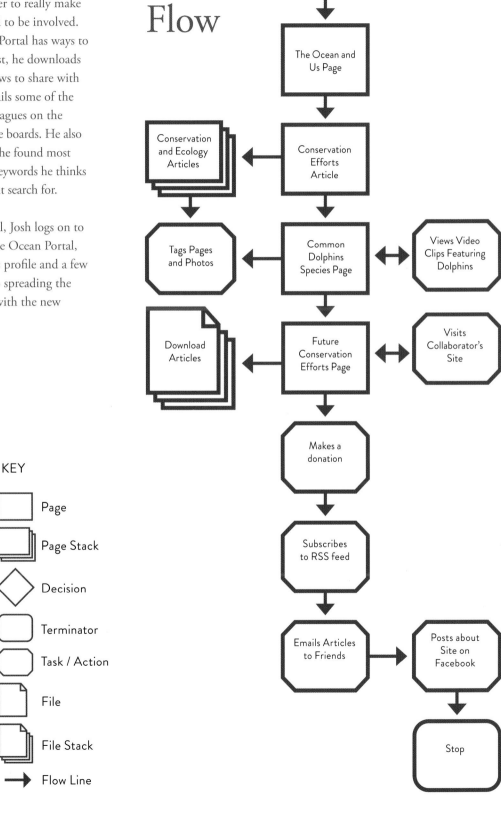

Josh's User Flow

Start: Link in E-mail

The Ocean and Us Page

Conservation and Ecology Articles

Conservation Efforts Article

Common Dolphins Species Page

Tags Pages and Photos

Views Video Clips Featuring Dolphins

Future Conservation Efforts Page

Download Articles

Visits Collaborator's Site

Makes a donation

Subscribes to RSS feed

Emails Articles to Friends

Posts about Site on Facebook

Stop

KEY

Page

Page Stack

Decision

Terminator

Task / Action

File

File Stack

Flow Line

Photo by Kevin C. Downs

Persona 3:

The Ocean Enthusiast

Name:

Fred

Background:

In his spare time, Fred enjoys sailing and photography. In recent years he has been very concerned about overfishing and pollution.

Needs:

Information on the current state of the ocean and tips on ways he can make a difference.

"I try to spend as much of my free time in the water as I can. It's so peaceful and mysterious. I want the generations that come after me to share in that feeling."

Fred's Scenario

Fred is chatting with some friends on Facebook. He sees that Josh, one of his friends with similar interests, has recently posted about something called The Ocean Portal. Curious, he clicks on the link and it takes him to The Ocean Portal home page. Not knowing exactly what he wants to do first, Fred tries the search box and types in "Great Barrier Reef," wondering if the site has pictures of the ocean area he knows best. The search returns pages about the reef and its ecology, as well as photographs, and even better...videos! Fred had already collected a good deal of media covering the Reef, but finds even more here than he had previously found.

Excited by what he was able to uncover with his first search, Fred tries searching for his real interest, historical information about ocean exploration. He tries "exploration history" and finds that a scientist recently published research on that exact topic. Fred reads the summary of the research and downloads the full article to read later. He wonders if this same scientist has done anything else on the topic, so he spends some time on an Ocean Science page related to the scientist's research. He spends a while reading more and then adds a comment to one of the articles.

One of the biggest problems Fred has always had in studying the history of exploration is that it's hard to mentally picture information that covers such a large span of time. He sees that there's a section called "The Ocean Over Time," which seems too good to be true. Clicking over, he's impressed by the wealth of information about the ocean's past, present, and future. He finds an interactive timeline of voyages across the sea that clearly and concisely covers the chronology. "This is so interesting!" he thinks. "Maybe I'm more interested in the ocean than I thought I was."

Along the way, Fred stumbles upon information about one of the sea creatures he loves to eat—the Chilean sea bass. Looking at the page, he realizes that not only is the fish actually named the Patagonian Toothfish, but also sustainability issues could soon mean less of his favorite delicacy. Suddenly, discussions about the environment seem to hit a little more close to home.

Fred's conclusion is that The Ocean Portal is a great, easy way to learn about any ocean-related topic. As he does with every site he approves of, he saves a bookmark to Del.icio.us and gives the site a thumbs up for Digg. He then takes out his phone and tweets about his day's Internet research on Twitter. His interest piqued, he starts searching around Twitter and some of his other favorite communication sites to see who else is talking about ocean issues, and if he can join in the conversation.

Fred's User Flow

Start: Facebook Link

Ocean Portal Homepage

Ocean Exploration Article 1

Download Articles

Comments

Ocean Science Page

Ocean Exploration Article 2

Uses Other Timelines

Uses Interactive Exploration Timeline

Ocean Exploration Article 3

Patagonian Toothfish Species Page

Posts about Site on Digg and Del.icio.us

Tweets on Twitter

Searches for Related Topics on the Internet

Stop

KEY

Page

Page Stack

Decision

Terminator

Task / Action

File

File Stack

Flow Line

TRY IT:

CREATING YOUR OWN USER PERSONAS, SCENARIOS, AND USE CASES.

Start by describing someone you know. What is their name? How old are they? What are their interests? How technically adept are they?

Now tell a story of this person interacting with a website like Facebook, or Google. Why do they visit the site? What do they do there?

Next write the concise set of steps necessary for them to complete a task with the site, like registering for an account, or performing a search.

Finally, draw a flow chart of each page they visit, each action they take, and each decision they, or the website, makes.

Here's an example to get you started. In it, our persona, Anna, requests a friend on a social networking site, like Facebook.

The following example helps visualize what user flow looks like based on the familiar action of requesting a friend on a social networking site.

ANNA'S SCENARIO

Background: Anna Bell is a twenty-four-year-old female from Chicago. She enjoys cycling and cooking shows. Anna uses this site to meet new people and to connect with old friends.

Anna logs in to the website. On her friend Lucy's profile feed, she notices that Lucy recently became friends with their mutual friend from high school, Andrea. Anna decides to request Andrea as a friend. Anna clicks Andrea's user name and goes to her profile page. From there, she clicks the "Add Friend" button on the left side.

ANNA'S USER FLOW

This flow (right) helps illustrate the steps Anna needs to take in order to add a friend and the potential responses from the system.

Now, try your own. Write a persona for a friend or your parents. Imagine them interacting with their favorite site, and write a scenario and use case.

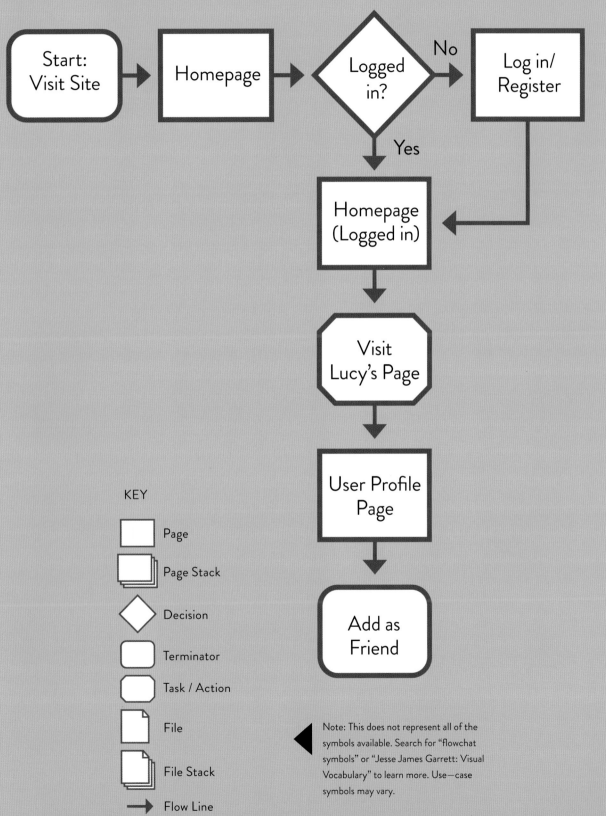

Start:
Visit Site

Homepage

Logged in?

No

Log in/
Register

Yes

Homepage
(Logged in)

Visit
Lucy's Page

User Profile
Page

Add as
Friend

KEY

Page

Page Stack

Decision

Terminator

Task / Action

File

File Stack

Flow Line

Note: This does not represent all of the symbols available. Search for "flowchat symbols" or "Jesse James Garrett: Visual Vocabulary" to learn more. Use—case symbols may vary.

Accessibility

Accessibility is a very important consideration in UX design, and yet it is rarely discussed in design meetings. *Accessibility* is a term used to describe how useable and accessible a website is to as broad a range of of people as possible.

Accessibility focuses on people with disabilities, or special needs, many who use special technologies such as screen readers, which convert text into speech, to experience the sites that we design.

The concept of accessibility in interaction design asks the question, can all our different users, regardless of their disabilities or special needs, meet the needs and goals that we have designed for effectively, efficiently, and satisfyingly? This worthy goal is often difficult to achieve, especially because designers are rarely trained in how to make their designs accessible, or even that accessibility is something they should think about.

Like all aspects of user-centered design, the first step in incorporating accessibility into a design is to understand the needs of the users. What are their constraints, how do they interact with what we design, what are their needs and wants? By answering these questions, we as designers can begin to understand how to make our designs more accessible.

Once we've determined our users' needs, there are many resources for designers and developers that offer strategies and tactics for how to make a site more accessible.

The World Wide Web Consortium (W3C), an international community that works to develop web standards, has formed the Web Accessibility Initiative (WAI), which develops strategies, guidelines, and resources to help make the web accessible to people with disabilities.
www.w3.org/WAI/

The United States federal government is required by Section 508 of the Rehabilitation Act to ensure that all U.S. federal information technologies are accessible, or "508 compliant." The Section 508 website is an invaluable resource for accessibility information.
www.section508.gov/

"Accessibility is not specific to any device, system, or platform. It is driven by an understanding of behavior, the business climate in which that behavior resides, and the social responsibility to manifest a common good. Accommodating people's diverse needs is at the heart of any inclusive design practice."

Kel Smith,
principal, Anikto LLC

Know Your Competitors

Understanding your client's goals, your users' goals, and the technology you will use to build what you design may seem to guarantee a successful end product. It's not, because you aren't the only designer who is trying to create something that will give your users what they want or need.

Your design will compete with myriad other products for your users' attention, time, and loyalty. This is true even if you are technically "first to market," and are creating something no one has ever seen before—a product that creates its own unique category, such as the micro blogging platform Twitter.

When Twitter launched, it had the unenviable position of having to not only explain what it was, and why it was different, but it also had to compete with a variety of other existing communication platforms and tools—text messaging, email, instant messaging, blogging tools, and social networks. Twitter's competitors even include traditional forms of communication such as one-on-one conversation, graffiti, and shouting on street corners.

By understanding and listening to their users, and by understanding the entities competing for their users' attention, the team at Twitter could make design choices that ended up differentiating Twitter from the other communication options. By understanding their users' evolving needs, and how the competing communication platforms couldn't meet them, Twitter, which started as a way to send text messages to more than one person at a time for free, ended up becoming something new and unique. It wasn't texting, or instant messaging, or blogging, or email. It is Twitter.

Behind the Bones

by Mike Kern, Partner, president, Welikesmall

Smokey Bones is a large restaurant chain with outlets all over the United States. They came to us to help them redefine their online brand, as they made the switch from traditional BBQ joints to edgy sports bars.

Continued on page 76.

FIRE UP THE
GOOD TIMES

Smokey Bones isn't your ordinary eatery. It's a bar & fire grill where big, bold flavors, hand-crafted cocktails and good times are guaranteed. So go ahead, take a look around. You're gonna like what you see.

LIKE US ON FACEBOOK ⊕
C'mon. You know you want to write "first" on all of our status updates.

FIND YOUR LOCATION ⊕
Find your home bones and like their facebook places page for local updates.

JOIN THE BONES CLUB ⊕
You get rewarded for eating and drinking. Why on earth wouldn't you

---

SMOKEY BONES

Competitor Site Analysis (in Casual Dining)

GOAL OR TARGET

COMPLEX

DEVELOPMENT

Technical Achievement and/or Merit

SIMPLE

⊙ Smokey Bones

⊙ Chipotle

⊙ Applebees

⊙ Hard Rock Cafe   ⊙ Macaroni Grill

⊙ PF Changs
⊙ The Cheesecake Factory
⊙ Maggiano's
⊙ TGI Fridays

⊙ Olive Garden
⊙ Hooters
⊙ Rainforest Cafe   ⊙ California Pizza Kitchen
⊙ The Capital Grille   ⊙ Benihana
⊙ Red Lobster

⊙ Longhorn Steakhouse
⊙ Outback Steakhouse   ⊙ Ruby Tuesday

⊙ Bahama Breeze
⊙ Johnny Rockets
⊙ The Old Spaghetti Factory

BAD   INDIFFERENT   GOOD

WHERE DOES SMOKEY BONES FIT?

DESIGN QUALITATIVE PROPERTIES

UI, TYPOGRAPHY, GRID, ETC.

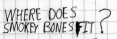

FIND YOUR HOME BONES
BONES LOCATOR

Looking for a good time? Stick your Zip in the box below and we'll show you where to find it.

Enter your State, City or Zip ⊕

What are you competing for?

The first step is to determine what your users want or need. Is it their time? Their money? Their loyalty? Are you competing to entertain them? To inform them? To help them?

It is important to understand the specifics of what your users want. For example, they may want to find a movie that's playing nearby, and starting soon—but it's equally important to understand what motivates this user—do they want to be entertained or waste some time?

In the case of a user looking for a movie because they want to be entertained, there are many direct competitors—applications such as Fandango, search engines like Yahoo!, and even traditional media like newspaper movie listings. Indirect competitors try to meet the users' motivating want, in this case, to be entertained. Indirect competitors for your movie app could include a bar or restaurant, a video game, or a sporting event.

By understanding the specific wants of your users, you can begin to understand the different options a user has in meeting them. You can begin to define your competitors.

> **TIP** Try turning your competitors into allies. Depending on the nature of your product, you may be able to offer competitors space on your site as a guest blogger or potentially share content.

BEHIND THE BONES

Want to get to know us better, like who we are, what we believe and why we're so awesome? Or perhaps you'd like to contact us, read recent press or take our guest satisfaction survey? Do all that and more by clicking below.

COMPANY STUFF

Continued from page 74.

We identified several holes in the interactive competitors within the casual dining space that gave us a distinct advantage when designing and developing what was to become a new paradigm for restaurant websites. Here are the advantages we identified:

Development-agnostic design: Don't be tied to a particular technology. Always use what will be advantageous when rapidly prototyping and building a site. Have a resounding reason for the technology choices that are made, and don't let legacy systems prevent the best work possible. For example: Don't force a site to be Adobe Flash just to communicate one animation on a homepage.

Design influences everything: In the creation process of Smokey Bones, we learned about the subtle psychology at work in the restaurant menu and used that to our advantage. If the type appeared to be too fancy, guests will assume the restaurant is pricey. Horrible readability with bad line spacing may leave customers with a bad taste in their mouth. Striking a balance of good type design will heavily influence brand perception.

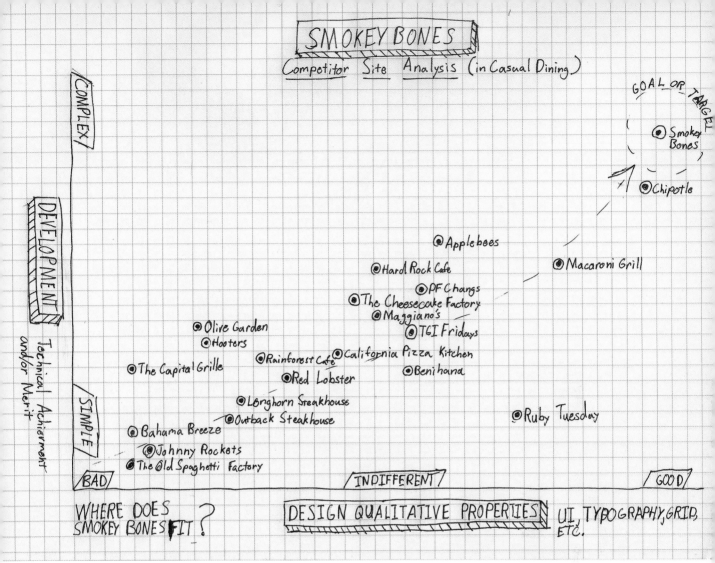

Smoking Bones competitive analysis.

Plan for the future: Thinking ahead enabled us to avoid the feature creep that often results in a hodge-podge of information on a restaurant website, and keep design integrity intact. We are always trying to future-proof a site so that launch day isn't the only day where things are perfect. We know we have been successful when you look at a site six months from launch and it actually looks better.

Smoking Bones website | www.smokeybones.com
Welikesmall, Salt Lake City, UT

TIME, MONEY, LOYALTY, AND ADOPTION

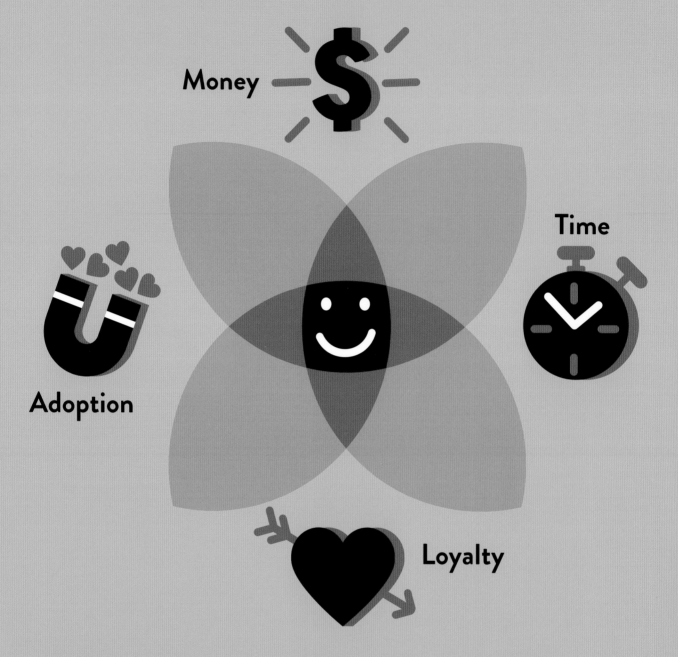

Money

Time

Adoption

Loyalty

No matter what product or service you create, you will likely find yourself competing for your users' time, money, loyalty, and adoption. It's clear what time and money are; loyalty and adoption require a bit more explanation. Loyalty is when a consumer buys and/or uses the same product or service repeatedly and is committed to continuing to do so. Adoption is when a customer's like of a brand is so great that they are willing to seek out other products by that brand. They have, in essence, adopted them into their life. When enough customers adopt a brand, that brand has the ability to control and define a product or service.

MONEY A band releases its new CD and you want to pick up a digital copy. Where do you choose to spend your money? Do you go to Amazon or iTunes? Or maybe you go directly to the artists' website or their music label?

TIME You are waiting for a friend at a restaurant and have a little time to kill. It's the perfect time to browse some apps on your phone. You could open any of them. Which ones do you choose?

LOYALTY You want to surf the web. Which browser do you choose? Oftentimes, people stick to one type of browser. The option to store passwords to frequently visited sites encourages this, too.

ADOPTION You just bought a tablet. You probably aren't going to get another one from a different company anytime soon. However, when you do upgrade, you'll probably buy a newer model by the same company. Your content and apps will likely be able to migrate easily to the new machine. And you've already demonstrated an appreciation for that company's products. You're unlikely to switch to a different brand at that point.

Competitive landscape

Understanding what your users want and all the different ways they can get what they want, is the beginning of creating a competitive landscape, which is a list of all the different options a user has to meet their needs—categorized as direct and indirect competitors.

Usually, your client will have a strong understanding of their direct competitors. A good starting point is to ask them who they see as their primary competition. Additional web research may be required to fully flesh out a list of direct competitors.

Most clients aren't focused on indirect competition, so it may be more difficult to define these. You may glean some clues from your user research. Shadowing can be an especially useful technique to see what other things may be competing for a user's attention. The key to developing a strong list of indirect competitors is to understand what motivates your users to want what they want or need what they need.

Competitive analysis

Once you've determined your competitive landscape, the next step is understanding how the individual competitors meet users' needs. What works? What doesn't? What's their unique techniques? What do they do that's the same as everyone else?

There are many ways to record and convey this information. Competitive analyses can be very useful in convincing a client to try a new direction or to explain why a design decision was made. But the most important aspect of a competitive analysis is that you, the designer, understand who the competitors are, what they offer to your users, how they do it, and, most importantly, how they don't.

White space

Understanding the competitive landscape, and performing a competitive analysis, helps a designer understand how they can be innovative with their designs by meeting user needs in the white spaces. *White space* is a term that's used to describe the things that competitors aren't doing and things they don't offer to their customers.

White space could be the fact that no competitor in the movie listing business tells a user what movie they can go to in the next thirty minutes. Or it could be that no communication platform allows users to broadcast messages to multiple people.

Mapping and understanding the white spaces around what you're designing is essential to making innovative design choices. Understanding what your users want, how those wants are currently met by competitors, and, most importantly, how they aren't, leads a designer to make strong, informed choices that are central to creating a successful design.

Are you ready to start making those choices? There's one more factor to take into account before you do—the platform you are designing for.

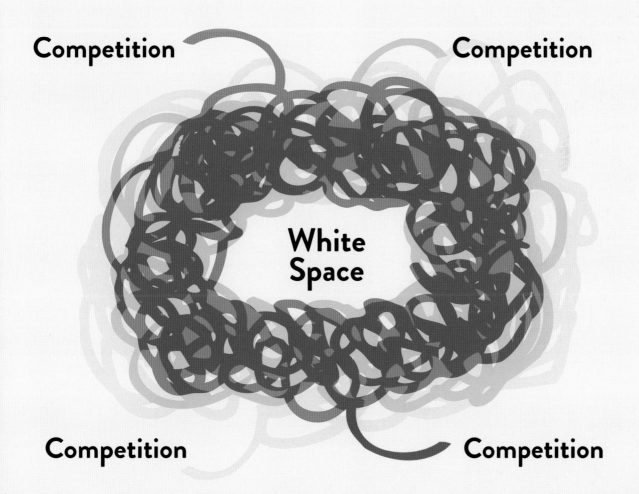

Competition

Competition

White Space

Competition

Competition

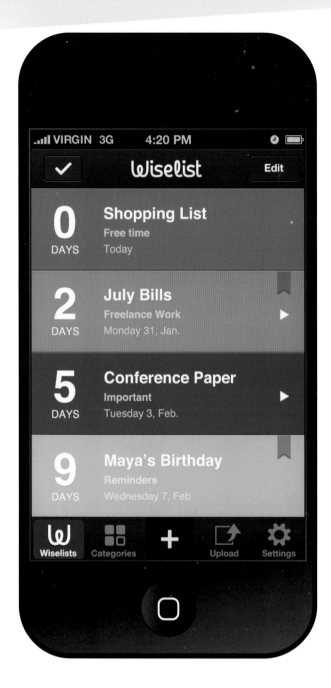

Wiselist app design.

Wiselist

Wiselist is an app (currently in development) that combines to-do lists and task management with data storage. With Wiselist, you can not only organize your personal and professional lives, but also attach the files you need to complete those tasks. All of your files and data are stored in the cloud, making you organized, portable, and productive.

There are a lot of effective to-do and task-management applications already on the market. There are also more and more options for cloud-based file storage applications. However, successful products manage to merge several tasks, thereby creating their own unique experience.

Wiselist

Things

Basecamp

Tickets

Producteev

Flowdock

Notes

Teux-Deux **iCal**

Wunderlist **Remember the Milk**

Remembers

Evernote **Dropbox**

iCloud **Amazon Cloud Drive**

SugarSync

- ● TO-DO APPS
- ● HIGH MANAGEMENT
- ● DATA STORAGE

By identifying the white space, Wiselist has carved out an opportunity in a densely packed market.

Wiselist App | www.wiselist.net
Wiselist, New York, NY

Content Is King

The primary purpose of many of the apps and sites you design will be to deliver content, including video, audio, photographs, text, interactive graphics, and games. Content that will inform, teach, or entertain. Content that may be created by your client, a third-party content provider, or even users themselves.

The best designs provide users with content that is easy to find, relevant to them, current, and simple to watch, read, and listen. To make good design choices, it is essential to understand what kind of content your designs will deliver, where that content will come from, how it will be created, and how often it will be updated.

Because finding and consuming content will be so integral to the success of the things you design, it is important to work with your client to define a content strategy. A content strategy is a document that outlines what content is currently available, what content will need to be created, how content will be delivered to the design, who will be responsible for creating and moderating new content, and how often content will be added and updated.

Infinite Creativity

Infinite Creativity is a multitouch experience that allows for the creation of collaborative, expressive, digital paintings. It was created by Second Story for Adobe Systems and the Spirit of Silicon Valley Exhibition at the Tech Museum of Innovation.

Continued on page 86.

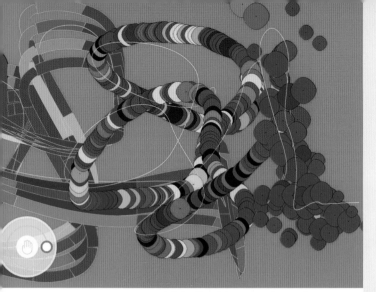

Infinity Creativity art creation touch screen.

Continued from page 84.

This interactive experience harnesses the creative power of exhibition visitors to generate a constantly evolving stream of art. Visitors use their fingers to slice and swipe on the interface, which generates squiggles, blobs, and ribbons of color. These are then broadcast to a large scrolling screen for everyone to view. This is a great example of user-generated content (UGC) since it is both simple enough for anyone to participate and engaging enough to capture the audience's attention. The content is also limited enough so that users can't generate anything requiring moderation, an important consideration when creating UGC.

Infinite Creativity Installations
Second Story Interactive Studios, Portland, OR

Why it's important to define content strategy up front:

1. Discussions about content can bring out different opinions from stakeholders because they have different agendas and goals. This helps start the discussion earlier.

2. Clients and agencies are not always clear on who is responsible for creating content. They may assume that a vendor is going to create a new piece of content and vice versa. There is usually not as much ambiguity with deliverables in other parts of the process. This is because new content requirements (such as additional video formats or image sizes, for example), are often identified after the contracts have been established. The quicker everyone gets on the same page, the less risk that the project schedule, scope, and budget will be negatively affected.

3. You will be empowered to make better design choices.

4. Clients may not see the immediate value of your services. In order to create a successful product or experience, you will need to bring a strategy to the table that can be built upon.

Format and types
of content

Content is the raw material that you will use to design your applications. Understanding the different types of content your design will deliver is the first step in determining good design choices.

You will need to understand the kind of content (audio, video, photos, or text), the format of that content (MP3, Quicktime movie, JPEG, or RSS), and the size and aspect ratios of that content (640 pixels x 480 pixels, or a 3:4 aspect ratio).

It is also important to understand if the original content is created specifically for your design, is aggregated content that comes from a different source such as a blog or third-party content publisher, or is user-generated content.

Recommended reading: Content Strategy for the Web, *2nd Edition by Kristina Halvorson. New Riders, 2010.*

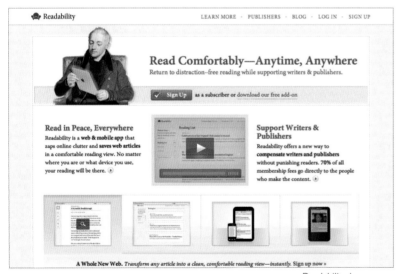

Readability homepage.

Readability

Readability.com is a web and mobile app that makes reading easier. It removes the clutter and distractions (like extra messaging, callouts, design elements, and advertisements) and presents only the article's text. Success from applications like this indicates that users are primarily looking for good quality content and often don't miss all the bells and whistles that traditionally accompany it.

Readability | www.readability.com
New York, NY

CONTENT TYPES

Users want good content, so it is important to identify what that content will be as early as possible. It's also important to identify who is going to be responsible for it: you or your client. The sooner everyone gets on the same page, the more likely it is that you'll create a successful product.

Here is a quick look at the major content types.

LEGACY CONTENT

Legacy content is content that already exists and needs to be incorporated into a new project (a redesign of a site, for example). The content should be reviewed to see if it should be edited, trimmed, or deleted. Ask yourself: Is it still relevant? What are its technical limitations? For example, if it is a legacy game, its game dimensions might be different than the new ones. How will the site design support this? And how will you move the content over to the new site? Identify what will need to be done manually and what can be automatically dumped via code.

CUSTOM CONTENT

The great game you made expressly for the new site, the pages of blog posts, the videos for the new video player, all fall under custom content. It's generally the most expensive to create, but it's also usually the best. Users prefer it because it is tailored for them and their tastes. And you know for certain that it will be on brand, because you're creating it that way.

AGGREGATED CONTENT/ PARTNER CONTENT

Aggregated content can either be automatically pulled into the site or editorially curated. Content that is pulled in automatically is easier to maintain, but runs the risk that it may not always be relevant to your users. You can allay some of this concern if it comes from a trusted partner, one that is in line with your editorial voice.

COCREATED CONTENT

Cocreated content is original content that is created with a group or individual outside of the client's organization. You do give up some control with this approach, but the cocreators often bring with them their own audience and perspectives, which helps to broaden not only the readership but also the editorial voice. Guest bloggers or photographers are good examples of this.

LICENSED CONTENT

Licensed content is purchased from a third-party publisher. This content can add depth and quantity, but it can also dilute the brand, as it is not created specifically for the users.

USER GENERATED CONTENT (UGC)

User-generated content is exactly what it sounds like: it's content that users create themselves. This can be an effective way for the site to generate new content, but UGC can also be tricky to manage and expensive to maintain. It often requires moderation, which can quickly become costly. And if users aren't actually creating any content, the site can look anemic.

SOCIAL MEDIA CONTENT

Social media content is content derived from social channels. This includes blogs, microblogs, social network sites, community sites, and even virtual worlds. Clients are often eager to delve into social content because it's trendy. But if they do use social media, they need to take it seriously. It shouldn't be used solely to push marketing material, and it requires that they take on a good amount of maintenance and new content generation to keep users coming back.

LEGAL CONTENT

The privacy policy and terms and conditions don't write themselves. If your clients have a contest, you will need rules, regulations, and other legal copy. Most clients will provide any necessary legal copy, but if you as a designer are creating your own product or experience, you may need to consult a lawyer.

The Process

If you are redesigning a site or application that already exists, completing a content audit is the first step to answering these questions. A content audit is an analysis of all of the content on a site. It most often takes the form of a spreadsheet, and it categorizes the content by type, format, size, location on the site, and origin, and provides an analysis of its quality. So how do you determine quality? Ask yourself: Is the content seen as reliable? Do the users read, watch, or share it? Is it actually relevant to them, or is it only on there because a client stakeholder thought it was important?

Content audits can be tedious. After all, you are trying to categorize a lot of information, so it's no small job! Get yourself a cup of coffee, then sit down, start your audit at a high level, and get progressively more granular.

Another important step during the discovery process is to get your clients' opinion about the content. This can be done through stakeholder interviews, group brainstorming sessions, or surveys. Get a mix of perspectives, from people at different positions in the company. Ask them: Do they think their content is meeting their business goals? Do they think users find their content useful or entertaining? Is anything missing that should be included?

Lastly, what do the users think about the content? There may be ways to look at the site data to help determine this. Are users sharing or rating it? Are they leaving comments and talking about it? If there are UGC tools on the site, are they using them? If they aren't, there may be usability issues with the tool, or they may not like the assets provided. Finally, go to the users themselves and ask them directly. Do they find the content credible and reliable? Create a survey or poll and ask them what they think. After all, the content is ultimately for them.

1. Analyze and plan

Once you have taken an inventory of the current content and gathered feedback from both your client and their users, you need to digest the information. Go through the content audit with your client and determine if their content should be left as is, updated, or removed completely. Determine if it is still relevant. Is anything just acting as filler, or does some of it seem outdated? Does it feel on-brand and maintain a consistent voice? Clients have invested a lot time and money in that content, so they may be resistant to editing or removing it. It is important for you to emphasize quality over quantity.

Part of your analysis should also include an evaluation of your competitors' content. What are they doing that you should be doing, too? What content is missing? As we mentioned in the previous chapter, look for areas of opportunity. Now is the time to start making recommendations. Earlier in the book, we talked about goals, users, and success criteria. Content needs to be aligned—or sometimes realigned—with both project goals and requirements as well as the users' wants and needs.

What you do with this information will have major technical ramifications. The first has to do with the content management system (CMS). Think of a CMS as a website designed for your client to maintain their website or app. Will the content be editorially or dynamically updated? Recommendations that stem from your content audit will likely affect the redesign of the CMS or the creation of one if none existed before.

Legacy content will also be affected. Legacy content can be ported over into the new site in one of two ways: via code or manually. Reentering legacy content manually is time consuming, however a set of eyes looks at each piece of content, so you have confirmation that it is working correctly. Porting over content from one database to another can be effective, too, and it is certainly less costly in terms of time, but the relocated content may not always display correctly. You lose a bit of reassurance by having code do the work.

Now that you know what needs to happen in terms of content migration and generation, you need to create a plan. Generate a timeline and schedule, plus staffing recommendations that delineate responsibilities for the various types of content. If there aren't those people on their staff (or yours, if you are responsible for that work), they'll need to be hired. You will also need a migration plan if you are planning on keeping any legacy content.

As you are designing the new experience, be sure to create word-count constraints for the various content blocks on the site. You'll need to be certain that the text doesn't run too long or short. Digital experiences are almost like living creatures, and new content is their food. So you will also need an editorial calendar to dictate when new content should be generated in the coming months.

Finally, you'll need a search engine optimization (SEO) strategy. We'll talk about this at length in Chapter 12, but for now, remember: You want search engines to find and index your content. So the content needs to be written in a way that is friendly to them.

2. Create, gather, and revise

Time to put the plan into action. If you are creating new written content, the writer needs to start working. Get any illustrators, designers, videographers, and photographers going as well. Managing this process is often complicated. Content generation usually requires rounds of revisions, with input from multiple stakeholders. Everyone from fact checkers and educational consultants to your editors and legal team, may need to give the thumbs up. And don't forget about your SEO specialist! All of this content needs to be created with your SEO strategy in mind.

If you have legacy content, start to gather it. Your content audit should have earmarked the content you're going to port. Legacy text may need to be revised to fit in the new templates and images may need to be resized. If they are too small to be resized, you may need to find larger images that will work. If you have video content on your site, but you've changed the player to support a larger viewing experience, you may need to re-export that video.

And pay attention to the tone of all of the content, both old and new. It needs to be a consistent voice for the brand.

3. Integrate and refine

Integrating your content is where the rubber meets the road. It is great to see your site or app start to come to life with real content. However, you still may need to refine your content a bit to get it just right. If you are aggregating existing feeds from another site, are they working properly? Are the user profiles porting over correctly? Are your legacy games or applications integrated with your new registration and log-in system? A lot of little issues will probably pop up. You should be fine though: Your plan has anticipated small problems and allocated the necessary time and resources to fix them. At this point, your content is ready to be published.

4. Maintain and revise

After a site is designed, built, and launched, its success will depend on the quality of its content. Users return to, and spend more time with, sites that deliver frequently updated, fun, informative content that feels like it has been personally crafted just for them. So how do you increase the possibility of success? Behold the content strategy and editorial calendar. Following it ensures that new content is continuously created and delivered. But you always need to look for ways to improve and evolve the content. Is the editorial calendar a little too ambitious? Can you streamline the workflow? Maybe there are other types of content you would like to explore because your users seem to want it? How can your users experience this content on a different device? Would the content need to change?

Let's take a look at designing for the right device.

IT'S NOT THE WEDDING, IT'S THE MARRIAGE!

by Kristin Ellington, COO and executive producer,
Funny Garbage

Everyone gets hyperfocused on the big date. Really, it's no wonder, given the time, effort, and expense that have gone into getting to this point. Stress, arguments, anxiety, hair pulling, and predate weight loss are all common occurrences. All of this drama and build up to create the perfect moment, the perfect symbol of what this entity is at its *very best*! Then reality hits the next morning, and you remember that this is just the beginning, day *one*.

Now obviously getting married is not *exactly* the same thing as launching a website, so why, you ask, am I likening the two? Because both are a very firm public commitment to grow, nurture, and evolve this thing you've created. And as tough as it is to get the wedding planned or the website launched, it's even more imperative to work on it, to keep it fresh and exciting. Unlike publishing a book or a movie, which is a full and complete statement tied up in a bow and presented as a fait accompli, publishing a website is a promise of things yet to come. Every decision you make sets the users' expectations as to how often they should come back and what to expect once they arrive.

What to watch for:

Free Content — Basic rule of thumb in life: you get what you pay for. Many a website have been planned with visions of user-generated content being brilliantly created by hoards of talented and motivated people. UGC is great, but you have to give the users a reason to be there in the first place, and even more reasons to return again and again. Facebook does this with massive amounts of new features launching constantly. Other sites do this by providing unique content that is used as a basis for the UGC. Remember, content, especially good content, doesn't just appear out of nowhere.

Overbearing Approval Processes — Many people fall into the "eyes are bigger than the stomach" trap, or more specifically, they want "everything and the kitchen sink" but can't seem to ever get anything actually finished and published. Know your team and especially your executives, and be realistic about how much, and how often, you can publish quality content.

Relying on Specific Talent — If you are relying on a specific person's talent to create content for your site, make sure that person isn't going anywhere. It is a much safer plan to create a style and brand guide for your content that can be followed by several people. Use that one-in-a-million person to create the brand identity or the evergreen content that can safely stay the same and doesn't require updating.

"Content
Design in the
content is

precedes design.
absence of
not design,
it's decoration."

Jeffrey Zeldman, founder and executive
creative director, Happy Cog Studios

Designing for the Right Device

The next step in the design process is determining what kind of device you will design for.

In the early days of interaction design, most of the projects UX designers worked on were for computers. We knew our users would be sitting down in front of a screen, with a keyboard and computer mouse at their fingertips. There were established interface elements, called interface patterns, which designers could use to present standard functionality to users. Many of these interface patterns were drawn from the real world. Buttons, which looked like their real-world counterparts, triggered features. Tabs, similar to tabs in notebooks, were used to organize information.

More importantly, UX designers understood how and when users would interact with the software we designed. We knew they would be sitting down, focused on what was in front of them. We could expect a certain level of commitment and attention. We understood how they would select a feature—with a click of the mouse—or enter information, typing it in with their keyboards.

With this information, interaction designers could make a great many assumptions about who the users were, how they behaved in relation to what was designed, and how they would interact with it. For example, we could assume our users were technically adept and knew how to use computers, that they were accessing the software we designed to complete a specific tasks, and that they were interacting with that software with a keyboard and mouse. There were some exceptions—touch screen kiosks in museums, ATMs, and early interactive television interfaces—but largely we could rely on these assumptions to help us make design decisions.

Forbes

Forbes, a leading source for financial and business news, collaborated with Gesture Theory to create their iPad app Photos & Videos. This app does not contain all the content from the Forbes.com website. Instead, as its name suggests, it pulls in only the site's latest photos and videos.

Continued on page 98.

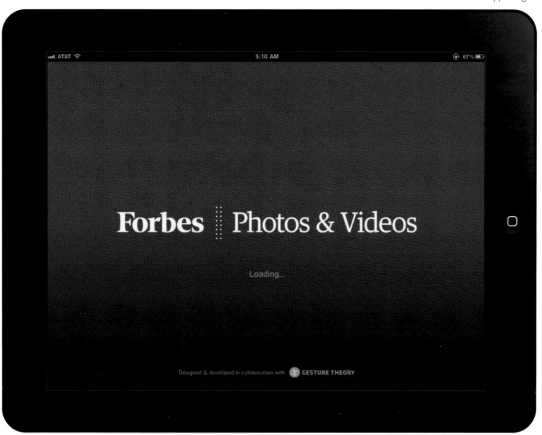

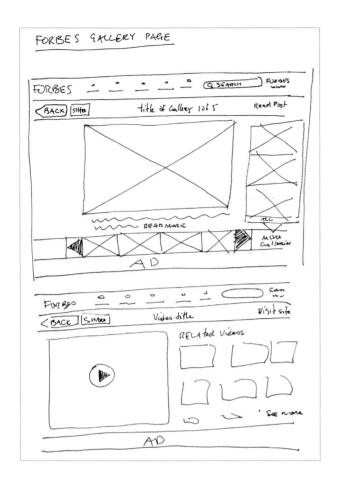

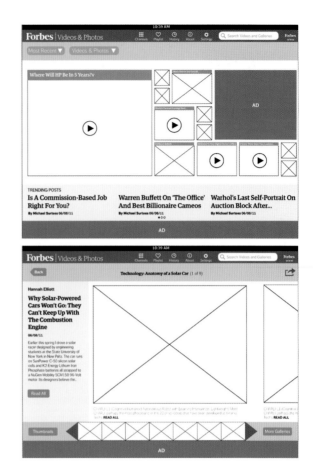

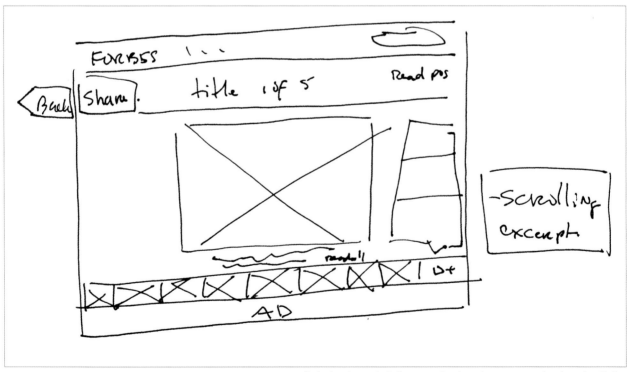

Early sketches and wireframes explore how the users can swipe through galleries.

OCTOBER 06, 2011

How Much Would Steve Jobs Be Worth Today?

By Investopedia

iPad (2010)

Critics laughed when the name of Apple's tablet was released, but nobody's laughing now. The iPad made mobile computing easy, accessible and fun --and brought publishers of print media clamoring to make tablet editions. It wasn't the first tablet on the scene, but it was the first without a stylus or a keyboard. By the end of

Read Related Post »

Forbes Photo & Video iPad app photo detail screen.

Continued from page 96.

This app displays a smart use of resources. Forbes is able to parse content from their existing digital publishing platform and reuse it to create a focused experience for their users. It also plays to the strengths of the iPad. The ability to swipe and tap images allows users to quickly explore the galleries in a relaxed position, rather than hunched over at a desktop computer. With its large, beautiful display and gestural possibilities, the Photos & Videos app is a great example of how brands can craft their multimedia to a specific device.

Forbes Photos & Videos App
Gesture Theory, New York, NY

Today's user experience designers can no longer rely on those assumptions. The world of interaction design has radically changed. We can no longer assume our users will be sitting down in front of a screen in a quiet room, clicking with a mouse, typing with a keyboard, giving the software we design their full attention.

Today, software runs on different kinds of screens and is used everywhere—in our user's pockets, in their backpacks and purses, on their televisions sets, embedded in our seat backs and appliances, and even in public spaces such as airports and city streets. They use what we design while driving, flying, walking down a crowded street, lounging on a couch, jogging on a treadmill, and in countless other places.

The way users interact with software is just as varied— with a tap of a finger, through voice commands, with a remote, through a keypad, with a gesture, by shaking the device, through eye movements, and, yes, computer mice and keyboards.

As the devices we design for become more complex, we know much more about our users without them having to actively enter any information. Using GPS, we can determine their location. Through on-board sensors, we can determine how they are holding their phone or tablet. Through cameras, we can track their movements or expressions.

Have you ever noticed a friend's email signature ends with something like "sent from my iPhone—sorry for typos"? Your friend wants to let you know that he is not stupid, but the device he is typing on is difficult to perform that task. Understanding what platform you are designing for—be it a smart phone, computer tablet, e-reader, interactive television, digital billboard, or computer—and in what context what you design will be used—on the go, sitting back, or with a group—is essential to making good design choices.

TIP As users shift from one device to another, don't try and mimic the experience. Create a new design for the experience that works on the device or a new look to enhance the existing one.

"A great experience has a clear goal. Different devices prompt different design decisions to accomplish it, but the goal should always remain consistent."

Jason Kopec, design lead,
Tag Creative

PRICE $4.99

SEPT. 21, 2009

THE NEW YORKER

PUSHING THE LIMITS OF YOUR DEVICE

Jorge Colombo has been creating beautiful paintings on his iPhone using an app called Brushes since 2009. All of his paintings are done on location, with no photos or sketches. His cover illustration for the *New Yorker* on June 1, 2009, made him the first artist to create a cover for a major magazine using the iPhone. The pocket-sized portability, along with the responsive touch screen has allowed Colombo to thrive within the limitations of the 2-inch by 3-inch (5 x 7.6 cm) screen, access to only three brush sizes, and no layers.

Colombo has since upgraded his Brushes app, allowing for multiple layers and more controlled brush widths making the process easier. He also paints on an iPad, but the experience is different. Just like a larger canvas, the wider screen is a pleasant upgrade. But since so much of his process is about being incognito and on location, the smaller, lightweight iPhone is still his preferred device.

The *New Yorker* magazine cover illustration.

Excerpted from *New York: Finger Paintings by Jorge Colombo*. Chronicle Books, 2011, by Jorge Colombo

"A technological breakthrough tends to be exciting at the beginning, and then it's just a footnote. Doing something early on isn't as relevant as doing something that will live on. We don't really care about who first used acrylic paints or camcorders. The same phenomenon will happen with the iPhone, the iPad, and whatever follows. Just one more tool. And it won't eliminate the tools that preceded it, either: Acoustic guitars didn't die when electric ones came along. Our tool kit is simply expanded. Using black-and-white film in 1910 was the only possibility; today, it is a choice, and thus has a different meaning.

"Until the iPhone/iPad touch-screen boom, painting digitally was for the most part an indoor affair. On a park bench, even a laptop felt clumsy, let alone one with a drawing tablet connected to it. The iPhone/Brushes combo turned out to be to digital painting what 35mm film and Leica cameras were to early photography. Lugging a high-end, large-format apparatus to a location is still an alternative, but the allure of pocket-sized equipment is hard to beat. Computer touch screens seem like an inevitable development, both as a future standard and as a common art-making tool. To me, everything else—keyboard, mouse, tablet, stylus—feels obtrusive by comparison, like a prosthetic."

See more of Colombo's work at www.jorgecolombo.com

Which device will you design for?

Initially, much of what UXers designed were tools that required training to use—including applications such as word processing or spreadsheets, that were used for specific, work-related tasks completed on desktop computers. With the emergence of the Internet, those desktop computers were used to consume content—find information, or entertainment—and UXers designed interfaces to make it easy to find and consume that content. The emergence of the mobile Internet and smart phones changed the interactive landscape again. Once again, UXers were required to design tools, but those tools were no longer just for work-related tasks, nor are they used by individuals who were trained how to use the software. Nowadays, you can design for many different platforms. So how do you determine which platform?

User needs and the context of where and how they will meet those needs dictate the type of device you will design for.

If a user is looking for a place to eat or a nearby movie that they can go to right away, chances are you will design something for a location-aware mobile device. If they are on an airplane and want to read, watch a movie, or listen to music, you will probably design for a tablet or e-reader. If they want to communicate with friends and family, you may need to design for multiple platforms, designing first for a computer and then translating that experience to a mobile device.

TIP New devices have the potential to improve the lives of people with disabilities. For example, tablet computers like the iPad are giving people with autism an opportunity to communicate and express themselves.

"To create a
feels natural and
to understand the
it's being used
in a living room is
an office or at

product that
ntuitive, you need
context in which
What feels natural
different from in
a public event."

Jennifer L. Bove,
cofounder and principal, Kicker Studio

DESIGNING WITH DEVICES

A quick reference guide to help you choose the right devices and design solutions for your digital experience.
by Kim Bartkowski

	Smart TV	Desktop Computer
	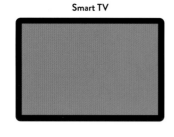	

USER EXPERIENCE

	Smart TV	Desktop Computer
UTILITY		●
INFORMATION	●	●
ENTERTAINMENT	●	●
PORTABLE		
CREATION		●
24/7	●	

TOOL KIT

	Smart TV	Desktop Computer
SOCIAL	●	●
ACCELEROMETER		
IMAGE RECOGNITION		●
GPS	●	●
VIDEO RECORDER		●
CAMERA		●
OPEN API		●
ADDRESSABLE	●	●
BARCODE SCANNER SMS		
VOICE RECOGNITION		
APPS		●
TOUCH SCREEN		●
AUGMENTED REALITY		●
NEAR FIELD COMMUNICATION		

CONTENT STRENGTHS

MATCHING DEVICES TO CONTENT

Smart TV	Desktop Computer
• MOVIES • VIDEO GAMES • PHOTOS • LIVE BROADCASTING EVENTS • LIGHT INTERNET BROWSING	• SHORT-FORM VIDEO AND MOVIES • CONTENT HUBS * RETAIL AND ECOMMERCE STORES • INFORMATION GATHERING • PLATFORM LEVEL DEVELOPMENT • HEAVY PRODUCTION AND CREATION

DESIGN ADVANTAGES

PRESENTATION OF INFORMATION AND DESIGN PRINCIPLES

Smart TV	Desktop Computer

• CINEMATIC DISPLAY
• EXTERNAL CONTROLLER
  (REMOTE, INFRARED, VIDEO
  GAME CONTROLLERS)
	• COMPLEX INTERFACES
	• CATOLOGUE DESIGN
	• NAVIGATE HUNDREDS OF ITEMS
	• EXTERNAL CONTROLLERS
	  (MOUSE, KEYBOARD)

When beginning to define a USER EXPERIENCE, most fall in three areas: utility, information, and entertainment. Once you've identified an area, you need to decide if your experience requires the user to input information (creation), needs to be on the go (portable), and have access to the experience at all times (24/7).

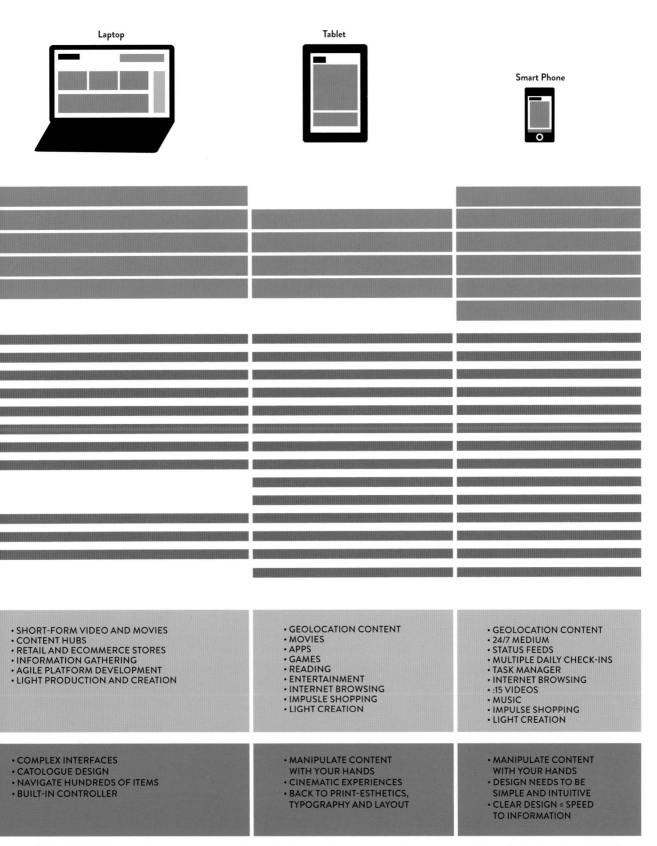

Laptop

- SHORT-FORM VIDEO AND MOVIES
- CONTENT HUBS
- RETAIL AND ECOMMERCE STORES
- INFORMATION GATHERING
- AGILE PLATFORM DEVELOPMENT
- LIGHT PRODUCTION AND CREATION

- COMPLEX INTERFACES
- CATOLOGUE DESIGN
- NAVIGATE HUNDREDS OF ITEMS
- BUILT-IN CONTROLLER

The TOOL KIT is a way to help you sort through the devices and technologies that are best suited to bring the user experience to life.

Tablet

- GEOLOCATION CONTENT
- MOVIES
- APPS
- GAMES
- READING
- ENTERTAINMENT
- INTERNET BROWSING
- IMPUSLE SHOPPING
- LIGHT CREATION

- MANIPULATE CONTENT
  WITH YOUR HANDS
- CINEMATIC EXPERIENCES
- BACK TO PRINT-ESTHETICS,
  TYPOGRAPHY AND LAYOUT

Each device displays and accesses content differently. Content is also consumed differently by the user depending on which device they are accessing the experience with. This chart is organized by each devices, CONTENT STRENGTH.

Smart Phone

- GEOLOCATION CONTENT
- 24/7 MEDIUM
- STATUS FEEDS
- MULTIPLE DAILY CHECK-INS
- TASK MANAGER
- INTERNET BROWSING
- :15 VIDEOS
- MUSIC
- IMPULSE SHOPPING
- LIGHT CREATION

- MANIPULATE CONTENT
  WITH YOUR HANDS
- DESIGN NEEDS TO BE
  SIMPLE AND INTUITIVE
- CLEAR DESIGN = SPEED
  TO INFORMATION

Some devices offer different DESIGN ADVANTAGES and are able to enhance designer experiences with higher display resolution, touch, and processing power.

snowbird ²·⁰

Snowbird Ski and Summer resort mobile app designs.

Snowbird

Welikesmall developed a mobile app for Snowbird Ski and Summer Resort aimed at visitors looking to plan a trip or visitors who are already there. The app is not trying to be a brochure for the resort, but rather keep frequent visitors to the resort "in the know." Real-time data feeds provide snowfall, snow depth, live weather reports, and information of any lifts or trails that are closed. The app also includes trail maps, up-to-date road conditions, as well as the ability to get directions from your current location.

The context of when and where the users will interact with the app heavily influenced the design decisions. Simplicity was a must since many users would be on their way to the resort, or already at the resort. Large user-friendly buttons and clear navigation ensure information is easily accessible, making sure users are connected, informed, and safe. The Snowbird app can be found in the iTunes store.

Snowbird App
Welikesmall, Salt Lake City, UT

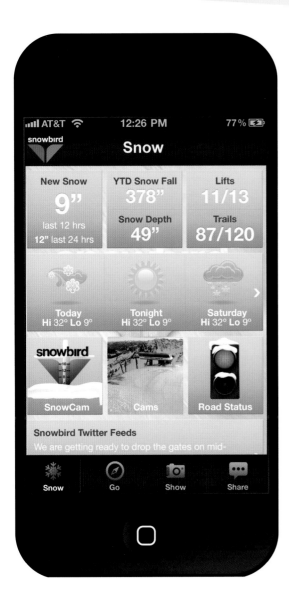

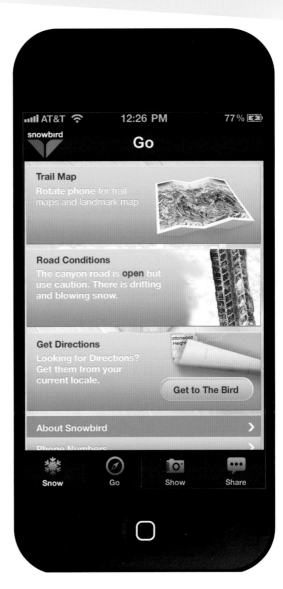

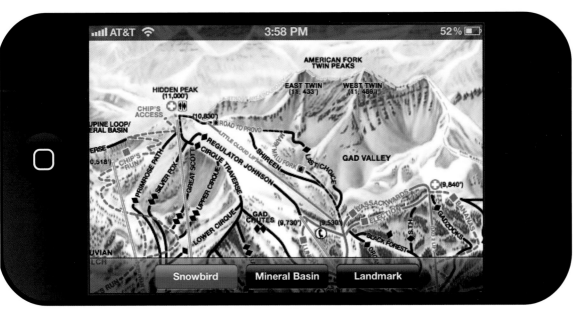

MOBILE FIRST

Designers are often asked to design a website first and then translate it in a simplified form for the mobile web. This can create a unique set of challenges. What functionality is left out in the mobile version if any? How is content translated to appear on a much smaller screen? Does copy require a rewrite? Are images resized?

A new design philosophy that has emerged is to design the mobile version of a site first, and then to add complexity, functionality, or detail for the regular web version. As mobile device use grows, eclipsing computer usage—in many regions of the world, more people access the Internet from mobile devices than from desktop or laptop computers—this becomes a much more successful design strategy.

Understand the device

Once you've determined what device you will design for, the most important thing to take into account is how a user interacts with that device. How they will navigate, and enter information. How big the screen is, and how much information can be presented and still be readable. A user moving a cursor around a 17-inch monitor with a computer mouse can comprehend a much larger amount of information, and can click on much smaller buttons or links, than a user who is navigating with a fingertip on a 3″ x 5″ (7.6 x 12.7 cm) screen. Data entry that is easy with a keyboard can be difficult when entered using a remote control or phone keypad.

It is a good idea to do additional user research once you've determined the device you will design for. Watch users using the device. How do they find what they are looking for? What frustrates them? Where do they use the device most often? What stops them from completing a task? How can you make their experience better?

"Brevity. Simplicity. Do one thing and do it well. Thinking mobile first is about all three of these. It's relevant information when you want it, and designers have the opportunity to curate a unique experience for products, brands, and services. Force yourself to focus."

Kim Bartkowski,
creative director

CHAPTER 8

Guide, Motivate, and Engage the User

Every day, there are more devices with interfaces that users will need to use to complete tasks and get what they want. To cook their food, they may find a recipe on a website, print out an ingredients list on a printer, withdraw money from an ATM, pay for their groceries at a self-checkout at the supermarket, watch mobile videos of cooking techniques, and enter time and temperature information into an oven. Each of these devices has an interface that a user will need to interact with. Interfaces that can be easy to use, fading into the background, allowing the user to compete the task at hand with a minimum of conscious effort, or they can be maddening, confusing, and feel like they are deliberately trying to hinder the user's efforts.

As interfaces become more ubiquitous and varied, and users are required to seamlessly jump from one to the next to complete tasks—guiding, motivating, and engaging users becomes a primary goal of good interface design.

Signature Theatre

Designed by Frank Gehry, the Signature Center in New York City is on its way to becoming one of the country's great cultural spaces. This collection of theaters showcases work by both emerging and established playwrights and enjoys LEED Gold Status, one of the highest rankings from the Leadership in Energy and Environmental Design ranking system developed by the U.S. Green Building Council. But what really sets it apart is the way the physical space encourages interaction between the public and the theater professionals involved in it. Artists, audience members, and administrators are encouraged to "collide" with each other in the venue's common spaces. Plus, the small size and flexible nature of the theaters allow for an uncommonly intimate viewing experience.

Continued on page 116.

Guiding the user

Navigating an application can be similar to navigating a physical space like a park or building. Applications have multiple "rooms" (in UX design we call them pages or modes), that contain specific information or functionality. There are different "paths" (buttons, links, or search boxes) that a user can take to navigate to those rooms, and many ways for users to get lost.

Users need to understand where they are in an application, where they've come from, where they can go, and how to get back to where they started. Good interface design, like good airport signage, provides users with signs and markers that help them understand where they are, provides them with enough information to know where a link or button will lead them, and provides them with easy ways to get back if they've chosen a wrong path.

Good interface design also takes into account that different users follow different paths, and have different strategies, to get to where they want to go. Some users will meander like window shoppers, browsing through the available content, before finally stumbling on what they want. Other users will know exactly what they want and make a beeline for it, utilizing a search box, or even typing in a URL to go directly to a specific page. And some users will directly enter from a Google search to a specific page, appearing as if by magic into the middle of a site.

No matter where they come from or how they navigate a site, these users will all want to know where they are, what they can find there, what else is available, and how to get back.

Continued from page 114.

Pop, a digital marketing agency based in Seattle, collaborated with the center to generate interactive touch-screen displays and several nontouch digital panels that add another layer of depth for the audience.

Several touch screens allow users to dive deeper into content about the play, playwright, or theater, including special commentary not found anywhere else.

Other touch screens encourage social interactions, connecting patrons in the physical space and online. They pose questions, such as, "Why did you come to Signature Theatre today?" Users are encouraged to answer via Twitter

Signature Theater touch—screen designs.

Signature Theatre Digital Displays | signaturetheatre.org
Pop, Seattle, WA

using designated hashtags or to interact with the touch screen. Both methods offer a way for patrons in the space to casually interact with each other as they comment on the responses of others.

Noninteractive displays found throughout the space offer directional and promotional information. They also display social media related to the space, including Facebook content and Foursquare location check-ins.

The various touch screens and noninteractive displays may not be the reason users visit the Signature Center, however, they provide another layer of engagement to the visitors' already rich experience and encourage patrons to return.

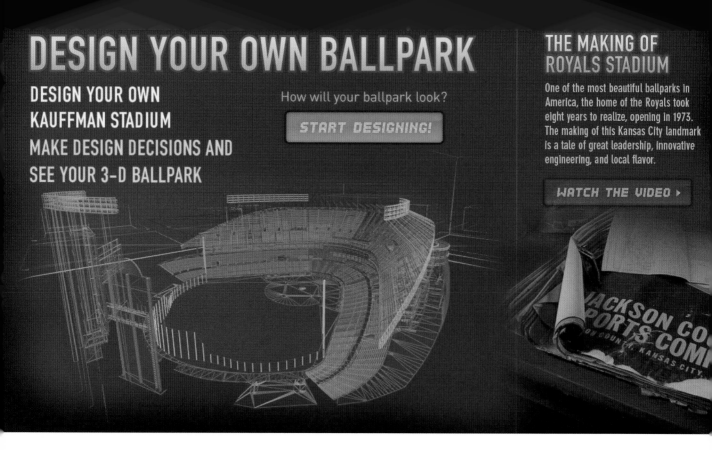

DESIGN YOUR OWN BALLPARK

DESIGN YOUR OWN
KAUFFMAN STADIUM
MAKE DESIGN DECISIONS AND
SEE YOUR 3-D BALLPARK

How will your ballpark look?

START DESIGNING!

THE MAKING OF ROYALS STADIUM

One of the most beautiful ballparks in America, the home of the Royals took eight years to realize, opening in 1973. The making of this Kansas City landmark is a tale of great leadership, innovative engineering, and local flavor.

WATCH THE VIDEO ›

Design Your Own Ballpark

Have you ever wondered what it would be like to design your own baseball stadium?

Fans visiting Kauffman Stadium in Kansas City, Missouri, are able to do just that. Created by Second Story, this dual-screen interactive experience turns baseball fans into stadium architects, allowing them to design and modify their own ballpark in real-time 3D.

Since the experience was created for the ballpark and not home computers, the expected interaction time was quite short. The product had to be deep enough for users to learn about the ballpark design process, but also simple and engaging enough for them to have fun and feel successful at it. To accomplish this, fans are guided through several small steps. Each decision generates real-time feedback, so that users can quickly see the implications of their choices.

How does the outfield wall distance affect seating capacity? As always, design decisions come with trade-offs. Revenue, attendance, and home-run percentages are just a few of the aspects that are affected by the stadium's features. Throughout the design process, users are presented with supplemental text and images from real-world examples, which offer more detail and insight into the many challenges architects face.

When users are happy with their creations, they are invited to show it off by emailing it to their friends.

Design Your Own Ballpark
Second Story Interactive Studios,
Portland, OR

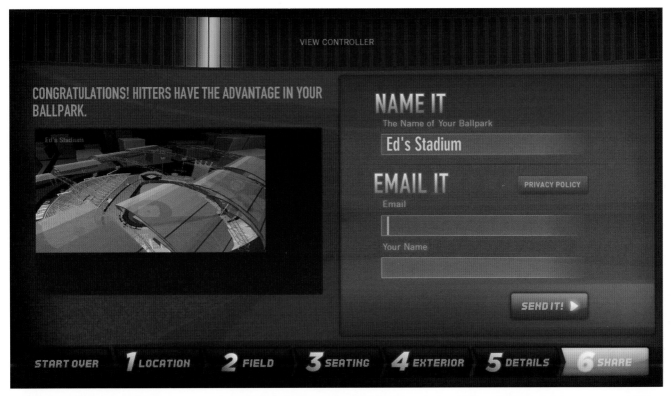

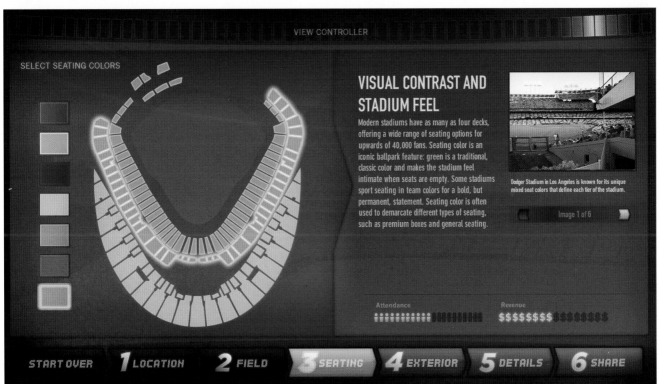

Design Your Own Ballpark touch—screen designs.

Burn Calories, Not Electricity

Take the Stairs!

Walking up the stairs just 2 minutes a day helps prevent weight gain. It also helps the environment.

Learn more at www.nyc.gov or call 311.
Made possible by funding from the Department of Health and Human Services.

Michael R. Bloomberg
Mayor

DESIGN FOR USERS' NEEDS, NOT THEIR WANTS: ENCOURAGING STAIR USE

In 2010, the City of New York released the *Active Design Guidelines*, promoting physical activity and health in design, which offers a collection of evidence-based strategies to create healthier buildings, streets, and urban spaces in New York City and beyond. Architects, urban designers, and real estate professionals can incorporate these strategies into their projects to encourage users to make healthier decisions. By facilitating opportunities for daily physical activity and increasing access to healthy foods and beverages, these strategies can ultimately play a role in combating the biggest public health epidemics of our time: obesity and related chronic diseases such as diabetes, heart disease, stroke, and cancer.

One example for incorporating regular physical activity into daily life is to design buildings in a manner that encourages stair use for able-bodied people, rather than elevator and escalator use. The *Active Design Guidelines* offer a number of strategies for promoting stair use among building users:

Locate accessible, visible, appealing stairs directly in view of the entrance and along the building's principle paths of travel.

Design stair environments that appeal to the senses. Incorporate interesting views, natural daylight, artwork and music, natural ventilation, and bright, inviting colors.

Place signage at elevators and escalators to encourage stair use for health and other benefits.

Design elevators to be less prominent than the stairs for people who can use the stairs, while providing elevator access for people with disabilities.

Consider installing skip-stop elevators, where appropriate for the building type. Skip-stop elevators stop only on certain floors, encouraging able-bodied building users to take the stairs to adjacent floors where the elevator does not stop.

To learn more, and to download a copy of the Active Design Guidelines, *go to www.nyc.gov/adg.*

This poster encourages people to take the stairs rather than the elevator to save electricity and promote a healthier lifestyle

WHAT IS GAMIFICATION?

Gamification is the integration of game dynamics or game mechanics into any nongame experience, application, or website. Users are awarded points, achievements, or badges to complete tasks. Sometimes, applications may use levels as a way to create a sense of status. Leaderboards show which users have used an application the most. Users are given titles like mayor or duke. It can be a great way to make applications more engaging, increase user motivation, and drive customer loyalty.

There is no question that gamification can lead to successful results. One of the more powerful examples is the frequent flyer program that United Airlines created in 1981. Many other loyalty reward programs have developed since then and have proven to be successful game-based business models.

However, gamification is not a silver bullet strategy. Not all experiences will benefit from badges, points, and titles. Applications that users come to in times of stress or anxiety, or for information that is private or personal, aren't fun. Clients often think if they gamify their experience or product it will guarantee success. In fact, it can cheapen the brand and alienate users if it doesn't offer any real value. It will also cost money and time to maintain the virtual rewards and achievements users will come to expect. It is important to work with your client and understand their motives and priorities and determine if gamifying their product makes sense for their short- and long-term goals.

To learn more, visit www.gamification.org.

I just got 200 points for walking down the sidewalk!

Motivating the user

Users often need to be motivated to use what you've designed. If an application or site meets a specific user need that can't be met through other options, then there is no need to motivate them. But that's rarely the case. If a user wants to find a good restaurant, for example, they have multiple options—from mobile applications to websites to books to friends. As more and more options become available to users, it is as important to motivate them as it is to guide them. Why should they select your application? What do they get out of using it? How will you motivate them to use what you've designed?

Users can be motivated in multiple ways—through rewards, through a clear understanding of what an application offers them, and through delivering what they want in the fastest, best way possible. They can be motivated by enabling them to connect to their friends and family—to brag or share.

Engaging the user

You've motivated a user to use your app, and you've done a great job guiding them through the experience. So how do you encourage them to keep coming back? How do you get them to spend more time with your app? Engaging users is critically important. It builds loyalty and increases the time they spend with what you've designed.

Users are engaged through entertainment. The more pleasure a user gets from interacting with what you've designed, the more engaged they will be and the more likely they will be to return.

Of course, fun and pleasure are subjective. There are many different ways you can add fun into an app—you can incorporate surprise or humor. Game play can be incorporated into an application to make normally tedious tasks fun like filling out forms. Good design itself can be pleasurable.

Determining the kind of fun that can be incorporated into your app can be a challenge. Humor works for some types of applications but not for others. Game play can be fun or it can distract from the experience. Understanding who your users are, and what they find fun, is a powerful way to determine how you can engage them.

Building Sitemaps, Wireframes and Prototypes

At this point in a project, you are armed with a huge amount of valuable information and insight. You've become acquainted with your team. You've learned about your client's business goals, the customer's wants and needs, what the competitors are doing to meet those wants and needs, and the content that your design will deliver. You've determined the device or platform that you will design for, and have thought through how to guide, motivate, and engage your users.

You understand much about the design challenge. Now it's time to design the user experience.

You will need to communicate a lot to your client and team—the information architecture or structure of the application, the content it will deliver, the features that your users will have access to, how they will use those features, what content and features each individual screen of the site will display, and how each individual screen links to the other screens of the application.

There are a variety of documents you can use to communicate this information—sitemaps, user flows, interaction models, wireframes, and functional specifications—but they are just blueprints. Design is an iterative dialogue between the designer and client and the designer and his team. Design documents provide a vocabulary for that conversation. Decisions are discussed, solutions proposed, and they are accepted or rejected. Throughout that process, the design documents will evolve to represent the current understanding of the design.

Of course, for a project to be finished in a timely manner, and on budget, those conversations will need to stop, and decisions will need to be made. Those final choices will be reflected in the last iteration of your design documents.

Sketch first

There is no one right answer to a design question. There will be many different directions and options that you can take as you begin to design a user experience. Some will meet your client's business goals better—and others, your users' goals. Some will work best with the available technology. Some will be easy to learn, and others will be more fun. Sketching is a great way to explore the many different design directions you can take. Sketch your ideas out with pencil on paper or a marker on a whiteboard. Discuss your sketches with your team and with your client—if they are interested in participating in a more informal design process. Sketching will help you explore multiple options and answer many questions before you begin creating formal design documents.

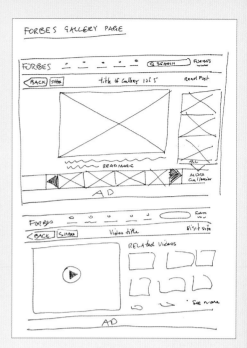

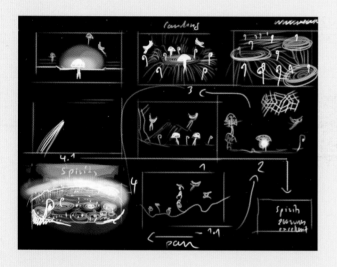

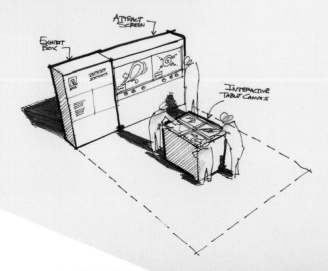

Sketch First
Examples of different sketches from several of the case studies in this book. The best sketches are quick, focused, and clearly communicate your ideas.

Interaction models

One method of sketching is to create interaction models. An interaction model is a simplified, hand-drawn sketch of a series of screen designs that illustrates a user performing a key action or task with the site or app. Interaction models are used to explore different options for how a user might navigate an experience. Interaction models contain just enough detail to communicate the core concept of the layout of the site or app, and how a user would navigate through it, to clients and team members.

These three interaction models demonstrate options for how a user could navigate, in this case, navigating from a picture of a cat to a bear. The cat is outlined in blue and the bear is outlined in green. The red indicates the users touchpoint.

 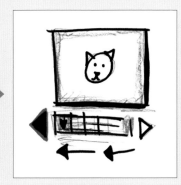 

Thumbnail Slideshow Navigation

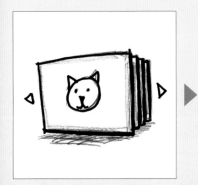  

Carousel Navigation

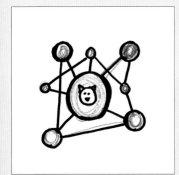 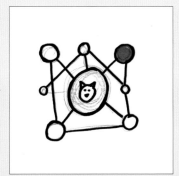 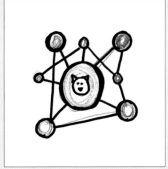

Nodal Navigation

The Power of Prototypes

One of the most valuable tools in the UX kit is the prototype. Prototypes are models or mock-ups of design ideas. Prototypes allow designers to test out their ideas quickly, without having to spend the time and money that would be required to build the fully functional site or application.

Many different fields use prototypes as a way to evolve design ideas. Industrial designers will start by sketching out their ideas on paper and then will shift to using modeling clay, found objects, or even 3D modeling software to develop the designs further. New technologies like 3D printers, which can "render" 3D models as real-world objects, allow industrial designers to take the prototyping process one step further and turn their digital designs into something a user can hold in their hand.

The goal of prototyping is to understand how users will interact with and experience the object, site, or application you are designing, and to use that information to evolve design choices before beginning the expensive and time-consuming task of development.

In interaction design, prototypes are called low or high fidelity. Low-fidelity prototypes prototypes can take the form of sketches on paper, or designs of screens (called mock-ups) using software like Photoshop. High-fidelity prototypes are interactive (also called clickable prototypes) allowing users to navigate through different screens, and can be built in anything from PowerPoint to development tools like Adobe Flash, and Flex.

Prototypes allow you, as a designer, to experiment and test design ideas. They make it easier for a user representative, or client, to understand design choices and interactions by making the design feel more real or realized. Valuable insight is gleaned by watching user representatives "click through" a paper or clickable prototype. Clients are better able to understand conceptual information when it is presented in a real-world context in the form of a prototype.

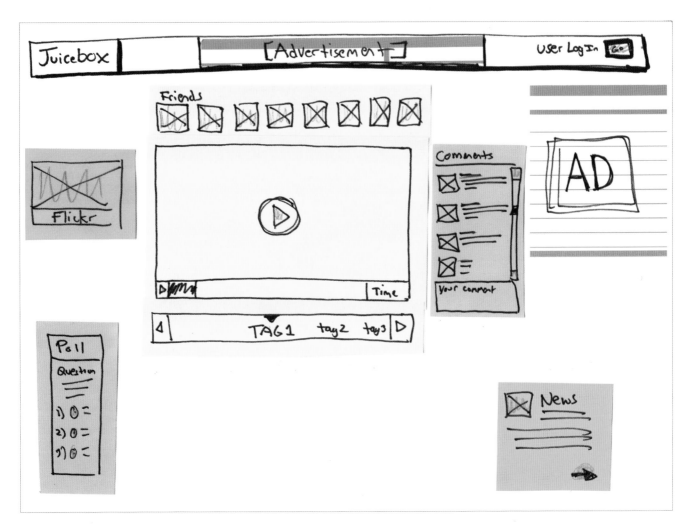

Juicebox

Juicebox was an R&D project undertaken by Funny
Garbage to explore the future of online television. Juicebox
enhanced a TV viewer's experience through real-time web
searches based on the show the user was watching. Content
from social networks, blogs, online stores, and news sources
were displayed along with the traditional TV programming.
Users could also connect and chat with their friends. The
ability to enhance the program, and to watch TV with
friends, made Juicebox a powerful social experience for
special events like award shows and TV premieres.

A paper prototype of the experience was created to help explore how Juicebox could work. With scissors, sticky notes, index cards, and a couple permanent markers, Funny Garbage was able to quickly illustrate the experience. Although the mockup was crude, it provided the team with a vision of what the experience could be.

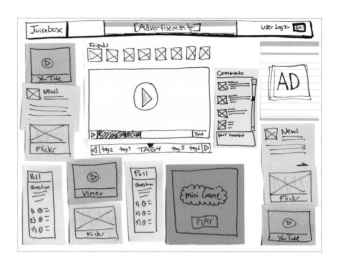

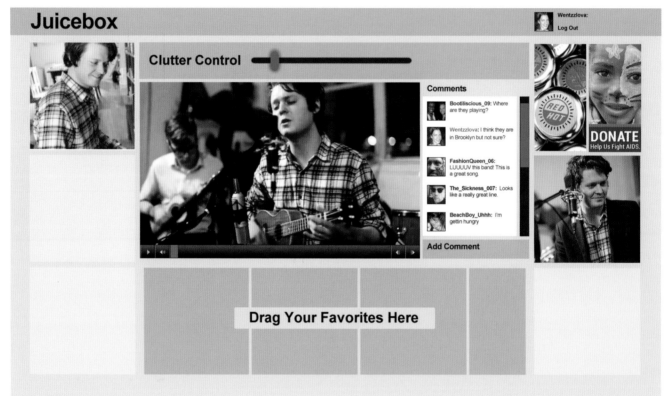

The paper prototype revealed two important discoveries. The first was that some users do not want additional distractions while they are watching television. They needed to add a way for them to control the clutter. The second was that some users might want to save content for later as the content was synced to the show, and sometimes changed rapidly. These observations were integrated into the next prototype. This medium fidelity prototype introduced simple interactivity, like the slide control, that helped users limit the amount of content that would be displayed. They also added the ability to drag and drop content to be saved for later viewing. The medium fidelity prototype provided a more realistic representation of how much content would fit on the screen.

The goal of early prototyping is to explore many different design approaches. By using low-fidelity prototypes, a designer can quickly explore different options. These options can be tested with user representatives and presented to clients. Using low-fidelity prototypes, a designer can quickly zero in on the design direction that is most successful with users and most liked by a client.

As an initial design approach evolves, design choices must be made to define the details of the site or application. Specific interactions and design choices must be made. High-fidelity prototypes help designers explore specific aspects of their design, such as how easy it is to understand and if it clearly helps users meet their goals.

Prototypes help designers test their ideas and make stronger design choices before beginning to build them. The more realized a design is, the easier and quicker it is to build it.

The final prototype was designed to feel as real as possible. Created in Flash, it played a sample video synced to enhanced content so users could get a sense of the experience. The content changed as the video played. This prototype became a proof of concept as well as a sales tool. It could be skinned for potential clients so they could see how the experience would feel with their content and branding. The three screenshots illustrate how the experience started out simply but grew more interesting as a user continued to watch the video and more enhanced content populated the frame.

Juicebox
Funny Garbage,
New York, NY

"We designed and paper
before we started coding
experienced in what could
are by definition capable of
paper or whiteboards to
equally true for some
users. In our case, it would
to program design ideas
feedback when we
half-baked!"

prototyped for months
Granted, the team was
be coded. Visual designers
imagining the jump from
reality. That may not be
programmers or most end-
have been very expensive
half-baked for user
already knew they were

Linda Holliday, digital publishing angel investor
and CEO, Semi-Linear

Sitemaps

The first formal design document you may have to create is a sitemap, which communicates the structure of the site or application that you are designing. Sitemaps show all the pages, screens, or modes of a site, or application, and how they are connected. Sitemaps can also communicate additional information such as which pages can be accessed only after a user has registered with the site.

Wireframes

Wireframes are blueprints of every page of the site. They depict the page layout—the arrangement of content, and interface elements such as navigation and buttons—and how they work together. Wireframes usually don't display visual design elements such as typography, color, graphics, copy, or content. They focus on what you can do on a page of a site, not what that page looks like. Wireframes should be designed just enough to communicate to your client and team the design choices that you've made, but not enough for them to misconstrue the choices you've made to also encompass the design choices that will be made by a visual designer—such as color, fonts, shapes, etc. Wireframes are primarily used by visual designers as a starting point for the visual design of the site.

TIP You don't need to create all of the basic user interface elements from scratch for your wireframes. There are many free templates, stencils, and user interface elements available to download to get you started.

SHFT

SHFT is an online media platform aimed at encouraging a more sustainable way of living through art, design, and video. Ludlow Kingsley, a small creative studio in Los Angeles, brought the project to life, doing everything from user experience and design to development and deployment.

HOME	SHFT TV	WATCH	SHOP	READ	ABOUT	PARTNERS	PRESS
MAIN FEATURE	ORIGINAL SERIES	ALL	ALL	ALL	ABOUT US	PARTNERS	PRESS CLIPS
WATCH		LATEST	LATEST	LATEST	FOUNDING PARTNERS	FELLOWS	
SHOP		ORIGINAL SERIES	AFFORDABLE	RELATED	CONTACT	FRIENDS	
CUSTOM		SUBMIT	PRICE RANGE	SUBMIT	CAREERS		
SHFT THIS WEEK			ASPIRATIONAL		CONTRIBUTORS		
FOUNDING PARTNERS			SUBMIT				
FOUNDING PARTNERS							
CONTRIBUTORS							
FB / TWITTER							
SITES WE LIKE							

SHFT sitemap and homepage design.

An important step in the process was the creation of a sitemap and wireframes. These documents provided the necessary information required for the client and team to understand the structure of the site and the general layout and functionality of the page templates. The documents were designed enough to be clear and informative, but were not overly designed as to suggest any type of look and feel.

The visual simplicity of the sitemap and wireframes provided the design team with not only the information they needed, but also plenty of room to explore various designs as these variations illustrate.

SHFT Website | shft.com
Ludlow Kingsley, Los Angeles, CA

SHFT
breadcrumbs >>>

Watch   Shop   Read   Category   About   Partners   Press

Search [   ]   Hey Stranger (sign up)

Shop

All
Architecture
Art
Business
Design
Energy
Environment
Fashion
Food
Home
Garden
Lifestyle
Music
Politics
Science
Technology
Sports
Transportation
Travel

CMS editor

Rotating Shop Gallery

Hulu style slider, preferably javascript, or code, no flash

CMS editor
Call out
copy with flash
transition fade in

1 | 2 | 3 | 4 | 5 | 6

Shop sort by > category | latest | Page 1,2,3,4,5,6,7,8,9,10   / Submit Product | Get Involved | Share with Friend

Title Sed tempor eleifend elit id lobortis. Sed tempor eleifend elit id lobortis.

Title Sed tempor eleifend elit id lobortis. Sed tempor eleifend elit id lobortis.

Title Sed tempor eleifend elit id lobortis. Sed tempor eleifend elit id lobortis.

fold

Title Sed tempor eleifend elit id lobortis. Sed tempor eleifend elit id lobortis.

Title Sed tempor eleifend elit id lobortis. Sed tempor eleifend elit id lobortis.

Title Sed tempor eleifend elit id lobortis. Sed tempor eleifend elit id lobortis.

fold

Title Sed tempor eleifend elit id lobortis. Sed tempor eleifend elit id lobortis.

Title Sed tempor eleifend elit id lobortis. Sed tempor eleifend elit id lobortis.

Title Sed tempor eleifend elit id lobortis. Sed tempor eleifend elit id lobortis.

Ad Space

SAVE 10% on
ECO Surf Wax

Title Sed tempor e
Sed tempor elei

Shft (c) 2010   About Us | Press | Causes |Contact | Advertise | Careers | RSS | C

SHFT gallery wireframe, and page design.

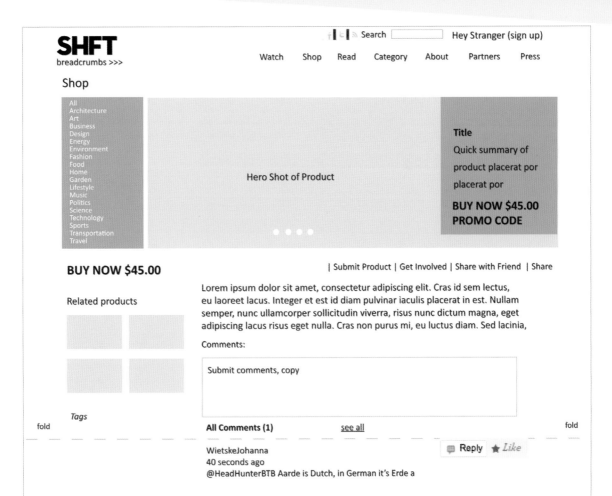

SHFT

breadcrumbs >>>

Watch   Shop   Read   Category   About   Partners   Press

Search   Hey Stranger (sign up)

Shop

All
Architecture
Art
Business
Design
Energy
Environment
Fashion
Food
Home
Garden
Lifestyle
Music
Politics
Science
Technology
Sports
Transportation
Travel

Hero Shot of Product

● ● ● ●

Title

Quick summary of product placerat por placerat por

**BUY NOW $45.00
PROMO CODE**

BUY NOW $45.00

| Submit Product | Get Involved | Share with Friend | Share

Related products

Lorem ipsum dolor sit amet, consectetur adipiscing elit. Cras id sem lectus, eu laoreet lacus. Integer et est id diam pulvinar iaculis placerat in est. Nullam semper, nunc ullamcorper sollicitudin viverra, risus nunc dictum magna, eget adipiscing lacus risus eget nulla. Cras non purus mi, eu luctus diam. Sed lacinia,

Comments:

Submit comments, copy

Tags

fold   **All Comments (1)**   see all   fold

           💬 **Reply** ⭐ *Like*

WietskeJohanna
40 seconds ago
@HeadHunterBTB Aarde is Dutch, in German it's Erde a

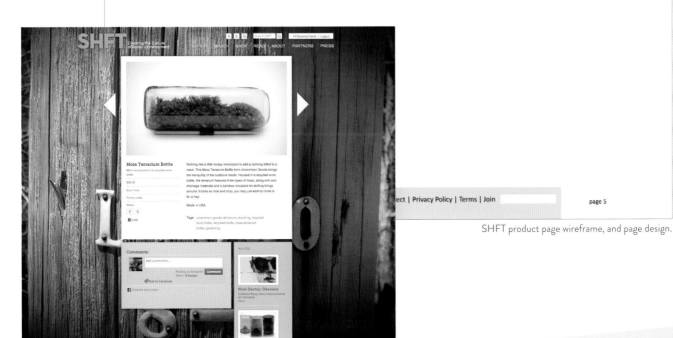

SHFT product page wireframe, and page design.

Functional specifications

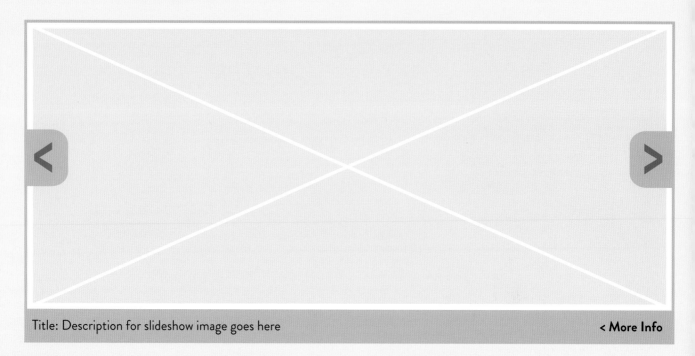

Title: Description for slideshow image goes here   < **More Info**

Functional specifications describe in detail what is intended to happen when a user interacts with the functionality or content on a wireframe. They explain details of what the designer intends the system to display when a user selects a navigational item or button. Functional specifications are primarily used by developers to code the site or application.

If you saw this hypothetical slideshow in a wireframe you would understand that the final experience should have a slideshow of some type. But the designer, developer, and client would have a lot of questions. What size should the images be? Can portrait-oriented images be used as well as landscapes? Does the slideshow support video? Does the slideshow auto-advance? Are captions mandatory? What is the word count of the captions? What happens when you reach the last slide? What language should the slideshow be coded in?

Adding the functional specifications helps answer many of these questions. The level of detail you need to provide in your documentation depends on the relationship you have with the team members and the client. Establish the level of detail required up front so everyone is on the same page.

Recommended reading: Sketching User Experiences: Getting the Design Right and the Right Design *by Bill Buxton. Elsevier Science, 2007.*

The Elements of User Experience: User-Centered Design for the Web and Beyond *by Jesse James Garrett. New Riders, 2010.*

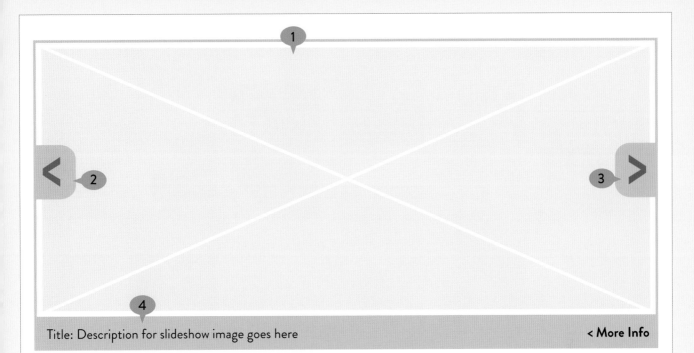

Title: Description for slideshow image goes here   **< More Info**

#	Element Name	Type	Description/Link	Additional Information
1	Slide Display Area	Graphic	Area will display 460 x 200 pixel images	If a portrait–oriented image is uploaded into the CMS, it will appear in the center of the slide. Background along the edges is TBD in design. Slides will auto-advance (and loop once the end of the slideshow has been reached) unless the user presses the previous or next button. See notes below.
2	Previous Slide	Button	Loads the graphic and accompanying text of the previous slide.	From the first slide, it will open the last slide in the queue. Slideshow will auto-advance until either this button or the next slide button has been pressed at which point the experience will be manually controlled by the user.
3	Next Slide	Button	Loads the graphic and accompanying text of the next slide.	From the last slide, it will open the first slide in the queue. Slideshow will auto-advance until either this button or the next slide button has been pressed, at which point the experience will be manually controlled by the user.
4	Caption	Text	Each slide can have a caption (title, description, and optional linked text).	If no caption is provided, the area will remain blank.

Real Networks TV-on-the-go prototype design options.

Real Networks

When Real Networks hired San Francisco–based design firm Method to help them design Tahoe, a product to enable users to take their favorite TV shows with them to watch on the go, Method explored many different interface options that users could use to navigate to their favorite video content.

Method explored five different interaction concepts through sketched interaction models. The models communicated how a user would navigate through the various sections of the app, how they would discover video, and how those videos could be watched on Tahoe.

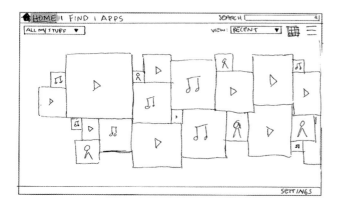

Interaction Concept A

Navigation / Home Screen
- Simple tabbed navigation
- Content is initially all of what the user has on the Tahoe, plus bookmarked IP content.
- Size, placement, and depth focus the user
- View and sort controls are also present to give the user more control on how to consume their library.

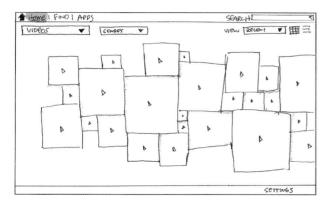

Filtered Home Screen
- On screen filters allow users to view a single content type.
- Size placement and depth are still used to give content importance.

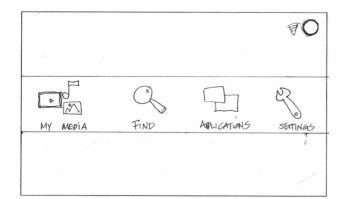

Interaction Concept B

Navigation
- Navigation is displayed upon powering on
- No home page
- Global navigation is accessed through hard button only.

My Media
- Displays media by type
- User can browse one type of media at a time.
- Screen-specific options are always accessible from the button in the bottom right corner.

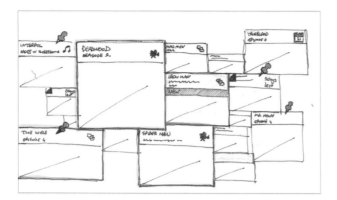

Interaction Concept C
Home

- Home experience is centered around media stored locally or immediately accessible via streaming.
- Content thumbnail sizes suggest relevance based on previous content consumption, usage patterns, and explicitly expressed interests.
- New content from a frequently watched series may appear larger, while older content that has already been viewed appears smaller.
- User can "pin" down any content that they want to keep for easy access.

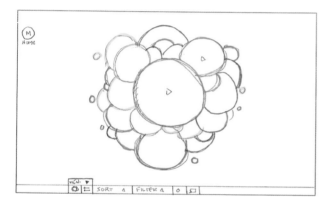

Interaction Concept D
Home

- Home is centered around the idea of a "cloud" of your content.
- Content thumbnails revolve around a sphere that is controlled by the user, as they touch and flick around.
- View, sort, filter, zoom and other controls will be available to give the user many ways to cut up the interface.
- Possibly through some touch gesture the user can expand/dissect a cloud to further view its content/pieces.

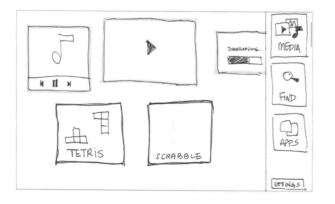

Interaction Concept E
Home

- Accessed by hitting hard button
- Home is like a dashboard that has primary nav, shortcuts to favorite content or apps, and access to all active tasks.
- This model highlights a feature that can be adopted by any of the concepts.

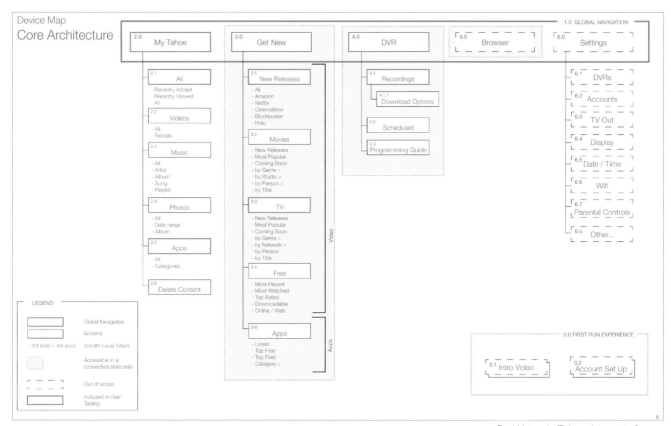

Device Map
Core Architecture

1.0 GLOBAL NAVIGATION

| 2.0 My Tahoe | 3.0 Get New | 4.0 DVR | 5.0 Browser | 6.0 Settings |

2.1 All
- Recently Added
- Recently Viewed
- All

2.2 Videos
- All
- Rentals

2.3 Music
- All
- Artist
- Album
- Song
- Playlist

2.4 Photos
- All
- Date range
- Album

2.5 Apps
- All
- Categories

2.6 Delete Content

3.1 New Releases
- All
- Amazon
- Netflix
- CinemaNow
- Blockbuster
- Hulu

3.2 Movies
- New Releases
- Most Popular
- Coming Soon
- by Genre >
- by Studio >
- by Person >
- by Title

3.3 TV
- New Releases
- Most Popular
- Coming Soon
- by Genre >
- by Network >
- by Person
- by Title

3.4 Free
- Most Recent
- Most Watched
- Top Rated
- Downloadable
- Online / Web

3.6 Apps
- Latest
- Top Free
- Top Paid
- Category >

Video

Apps

4.1 Recordings

4.1.1 Download Options

4.2 Scheduled

4.3 Programming Guide

6.1 DVRs

6.2 Accounts

6.3 TV Out

6.4 Display

6.5 Date / Time

6.6 Wifi

6.7 Parental Controls

6.x Other...

0.0 FIRST RUN EXPERIENCE

| 0.1 Intro Video | 0.2 Account Set Up |

LEGEND

	Global Navigation
	Screens
- 3rd level > 4th level	3rd/4th Level Filters
	Accessible in a connected state only
	Out of scope
	Included in User Testing

8

Real Networks TV-on-the-go wireframes.

Method created a device map to communicate all the different screens that would need to be designed for Tahoe. The map shows Tahoe's primary screens, all the secondary screens that fall under the primary screens, and additional supporting screens. The structure of the Tahoe application is easy to see through the hierarchical structure of the map. Tahoe's primary navigation is represented by the primary screens in the map.

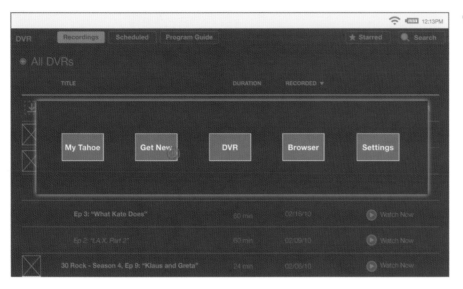

Global Nav

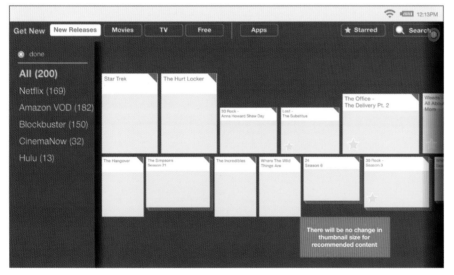

New Releases
- New releases can be filtered by source.
- Search can be accessible from My Tahoe, Get New, and DVR and is applied across all sections for each search.

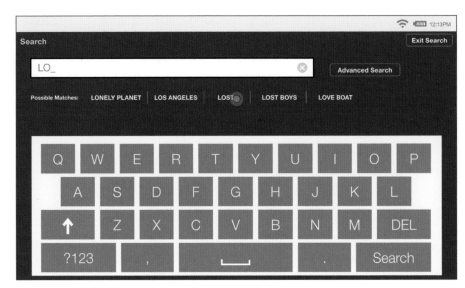

Keyword Search
- As the user keys in the search terms, possible matches will be suggested under the text field.
- Tapping "search" or a suggested search term will submit the query and load the search results screen.

Series Detail
- The series detail includes an option to record.
- Selecting the record option will open a screen with recording options.

For Real Networks' Tahoe, Method created detailed wireframes for every screen of the application. The wireframes clearly communicate the structure of the application, the content, and functionality that users have access to. The wireframes are designed enough to clearly communicate these details, which might have distracted from the design process.

Real Networks
Method, San Francisco, CA

Branding
the Experience

Now that you've designed the information architecture of the site—its structure, what content and functionality appear on each page, and how the pages link together—the next step in the user experience design process is to brand the experience, that is, to create the visual design of the site.

Branding used to be defined as the design elements—logo, packaging design, advertising, and marketing messages—that signified a product or company to consumers. The brand gave consumers an easy way to recognize a desired product on a shelf or to ask for it directly. As consumers grew more sophisticated, branding came to be more than just pleasing visual designs. Branding is now used to describe the emotional connection a consumer makes with a product or company. Fans of Coca-Cola love the soft drink not just because of the taste, or the distinctive bottle, or the red and white logo, they love Coke because the brand has come to represent a set of emotions and memories—nostalgia, connection, and happiness.

In the interactive world, brand is even more complicated. Author and digital strategist Seth Godin says, "A brand is the set of expectations, memories, stories, and relationships that, taken together, account for a consumer's decision to choose one product or service over another." In other words, a brand is not just the emotional connection a product triggers in its consumers. A brand is the set of promises the product makes to its customers. Google promises its users "access to the world's information in one click." Amazon promises to "provide friendly, easy access to products at a fair price." Anything less for either of these huge Internet brands would disappoint their customers and threaten Google's and Amazon's reputations, also known as their brand perceptions.

In the interactive world, branding has become user centered.

Cartoon Network App

Cartoon Network (CN) is an American television network aimed at children aged eight to fourteen. They also maintain a popular website, which includes cartoons, videos, and free character-related games.

Continued on page 148.

Cartoon Network iPad app design.

Continued from page 146.

Their audience is particularly tech savvy: around 50 percent own an iPod Touch, and most kids have access to two or more mobile devices. It was important to CN that its new app break major ground in this sphere. Given its users' love of both playing games and watching shows, it made sense that the app incorporates these two functions.

CN didn't want to change the content it offered online, but the functional capabilities of the iPhone and iPod Touch offered new and different opportunities for how to use that content. So a simple, but powerful, idea was born: Use the device's orientation as navigation.

If you turn the device counterclockwise, the device becomes a portable TV. Just like on-air and online, the device pulls in the latest and greatest video content. Users can see clips or log in to see full episodes.

Cartoon Network iPhone app in play mode.

If users rotate the device 180 degrees, the device becomes a portable game console. Custom games were designed specifically for this device, which encourage gestures including touching, tapping, sliding, and swiping.

The larger display of the iPad allows for the experience to be pushed even further. As with the iPhone and iPod Touch, the device orientation still works as navigation. However, when the iPad is in portrait mode, users can watch their favorite videos and play games at the same time. User testing revealed that kids of this age are often multitasking. So the creators paid a lot of attention to the types of games that kids would enjoy while watching a video.

The CN app is more than just the typography, animation, colors, sound, and design elements. It is more than entertaining shows and engaging games. The functionality of the app offers a new layer to the brand. It is both completely their own and speaks directly to their users.

The Cartoon Network app can be found in the iTunes store.

Cartoon Network iPhone app in watch mode.

Cartoon Network App
Funny Garbage, New York, NY
Dreamsocket, Atlanta, GA
All Things Media, Ramsey, NJ

CARTOON NETWORK and the logo and all related characters and elements are trademarks of and © Cartoon Network. A Time Warner Company.

Cartoon Network iPad app design.

The Evolution
of Brand Layers

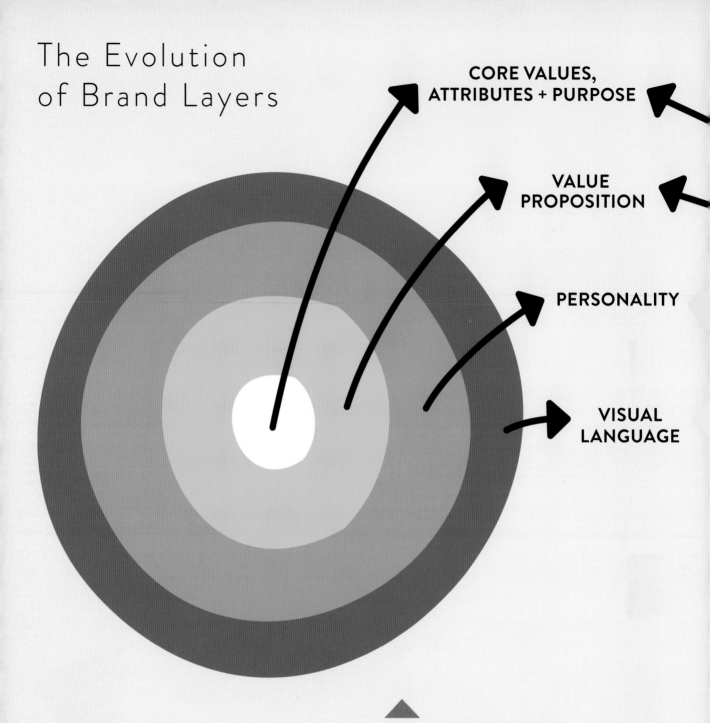

**CORE VALUES,
ATTRIBUTES + PURPOSE**

**VALUE
PROPOSITION**

PERSONALITY

**VISUAL
LANGUAGE**

Damien Newman, principal at Central in San Francisco, CA, helps visualize how the layers of a brand have evolved. According to Newman, "Today's brands exist in a lively world of stories, purpose, and meaning. People connect and interact with companies through networks and communities. New layers of brands are forming: The story interaction layer and the meaning layer."

Diagram by Damien Newman

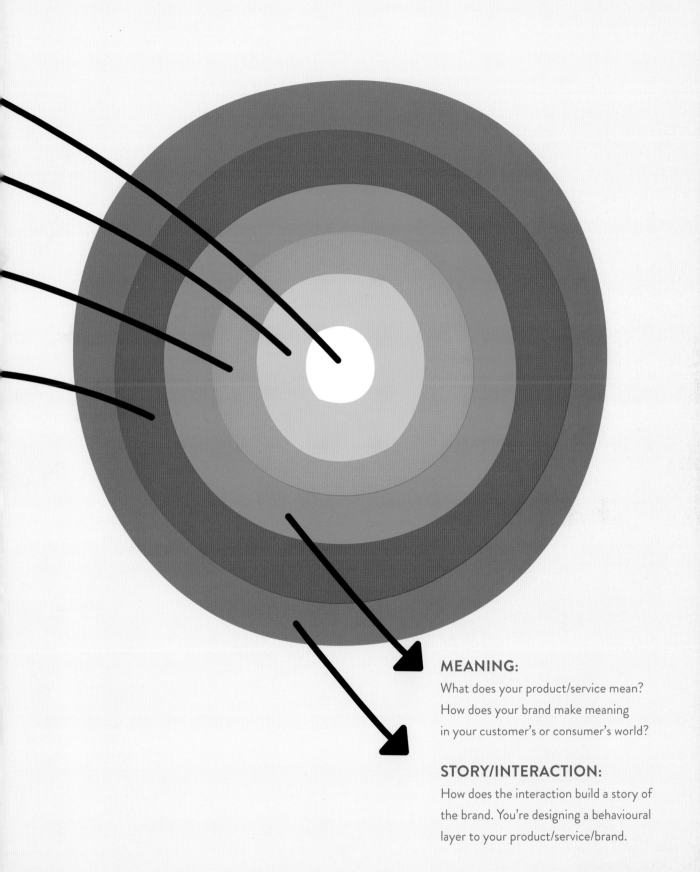

MEANING:

What does your product/service mean?
How does your brand make meaning
in your customer's or consumer's world?

STORY/INTERACTION:

How does the interaction build a story of
the brand. You're designing a behavioural
layer to your product/service/brand.

Personality

A product's brand is often described in terms of its personality. Is the brand sophisticated, funny, charming, or serious? If the brand were a person, what kind of person would it be? A hard-working partner? A fun-loving and funny friend? You develop an emotional connection with everyone in your life. Maybe you have a friend who makes you laugh because of their laugh, or a coworker that annoys you because of the tone of their voice. Brands also evoke an emotional response. There are probably brands that you love or hate, not because of the color of their logo but because of how they make you feel.

So if you break it down, the content of the site—copy, audio, and video—communicates what the brand has to say. The design of the site—color, fonts, images, and tone of the copy—communicates how the brand says it. The combination of what a brand says, how it says it, and how it makes you feel is the personality of the site.

The personality of a brand is communicated every place a customer interacts with or hears about a brand—in product marketing, advertising, customer support, and in what other customers have to say about it on social networks such as Facebook and Twitter. As the designer, you have the responsibility to explore and utilize these touch points to maintain brand consistency and personality.

We have finally reached a point where digital experiences are technically powerful enough to translate and enhance a brand's personality from traditional media without sacrificing project goals. Accessibility and searchability are a couple of common project requirements that would fight against a designer's efforts to maintain visual consistency. For example, advances with typography on the web have allowed typography to be stylized in a visual language while still being dynamic and searchable.

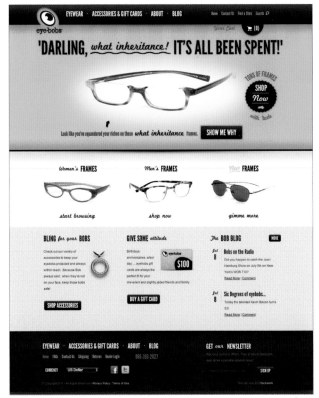

Alternate homepage header

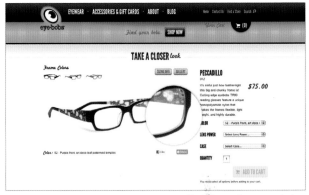

Eyebobs product page design.

Eyebobs home page design.

Eyebobs

Eyebobs is an online shop for reading glasses. Since this type of product is so personal, many people are reluctant to buy glasses online. Thus, one of Clockwork's main challenges was to design a site that was so appealing and informative, people felt comfortable purchasing the glasses sight unseen.

Eyebobs prides itself on being both hip and a little quirky, and the copywriting on the website reflects this. They knew personality wouldn't be enough to sell the product, though. So Clockwork used beautiful product imagery and stylized typography to bring out the personality of each eyeglass pair.

They also made the online shopping experience smooth. Navigation is easy, as is customization of the product. An intuitive magnification lens over the top of the photos allows users to see a great level of detail. It's as if they are holding the actual pair of glasses in their hands. This helps to allay some of the fears that come from buying a product like this online. Plus, visitors are allowed to checkout without an account, which speeds up the purchasing process significantly. All of these decisions help to make shopping here both fun and reassuring, which speaks to the goals of the brand.

Eyebobs Website | www.eyebobs.com
Clockwork Active Media Systems, Minneapolis, MN

Google™

Google

If you use Google's homepage to search the web, then you have probably seen one of the hundreds of variations on the their logo. Google Doodles, as they are commonly known, celebrate the major achievements of man, significant events, and notable people around the world.

The history of Google Doodles dates back to 1998, when Google founders Larry and Sergey gave their logo a little update to indicate their attendance at Burning Man. A small stick figure drawing behind the second "o" in the logo was their fun way to announce we are "out of the office."

Hundreds of doodles later, the Google Doodle is an important part of their brand as some users eagerly await the release of new doodles. They add a bit of personality to an experience that is largely technical and task oriented (like searching), and highlight the creativity of the brand. In fact, Google has a whole team of designers that create new doodles or work with outside artists. There is also a popular Doodle 4 Google contest open to K-12 students enrolled in any U.S.-based school.

Just like the company, the doodles are evolving. More and more of them are becoming interactive, offering innovative little surprises. Google doesn't have to invest in this constant reinvention of their logo. After all, most branding experts would never recommend so many variations and style. But that is who they are. That is their personality and it is important they showcase their creative and technical sides.

Google Doodles | google.com
Google, Mountain View, CA

160th Anniversary
of the first World's
Fair (Global)
This one is interactive.
Google it.

Earth Day (Global)
This one is interactive.
Google it.

Freedom Day
(South Africa)

Italo Calvino's 88th Birthday (Italy)

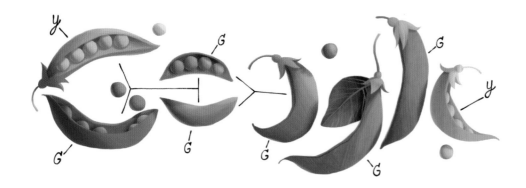

Gregor Mendel's 189th Birthday (Global)

Birthday of Katsushika Hokusai (Japan)

137th Birthday
of Harry Houdini
(Global)

Lantern Festival
(China, Hong Kong,
Taiwan)

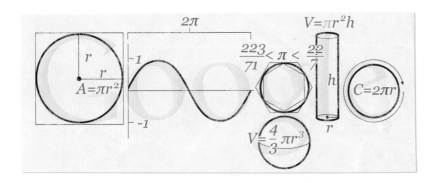

Pi Day
(Selected Countries)

110th Anniversary
of the Lisbon Tram
(Portugal)

Art Clokey's 90th
Birthday (Global)

55th Anniversary:
Rosa Parks refuses to
move (US)

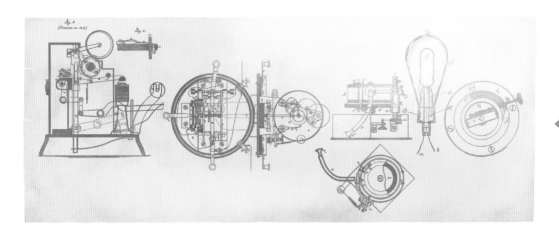

Thomas Edison's
Birthday (Global)

50th Anniversary
of the First Man in
Space (Global)
This one is interactive.
Google it.

112th Birthday of
Jorge Luis Borges
(Global)

HOW TO BUILD A BRANDED APP THAT DOESN'T SUCK

by Paul Pierson, partner and design director at Carbone Smolan Agency

When longtime Carbone Smolan Agency client Canon, U.S.A. came to us to design an iPhone app, we knew we couldn't merely showcase the Canon product line. We had to go deeper. Too many brands make the mistake of creating apps for promotion that merely tell people about the company. However, creating a successful branded app means shifting from telling to helping. Apps only gain adoption with users when they help consumers achieve a brand-relevant mission by creating a new experience.

Canon iPhone app design.

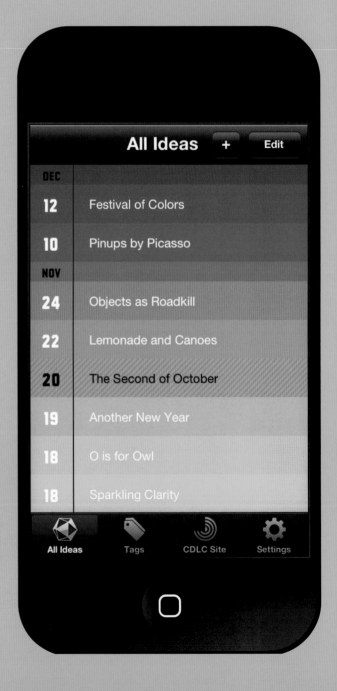

Step One: The Brand

The first step is to uncover the brand's core mission. This is often the hardest part, but brands with good apps have done it well. For Nike, its mission is to be fit and the app helps people run by turning exercise into a game. Whole Foods' mission is to be healthy, and its app allows people to cook better by providing a recipe collection and shopping list. For Canon, we found that their cameras inspire photographers to make the best possible images. We advised Canon to make their mission "be inspired" and their app, like their hardware, should help feed this inspiration.

Step Two: The App

With the mission in mind, the next step is to create a unique tool that helps people achieve it. How could Canon create an app that helps inspire consumers? In our survey of the app market, there were plenty of photo filter apps, but nothing that helped photographers create and pursue personal projects, where many photographers say inspiration originates. So we built an advanced idea-generation machine that can generate a virtually infinite amount of image concepts in just two short taps. Like the apps for Nike and Whole Foods, Canon's works in perfect tandem with their product line.

Step Three: The Design

Design is the last step: make sure the app passes the logo swap test. If you substitute the logo of your client with that of a competitor, it should feel considerably out of place. For Canon, the design of the app was crafted after the Canon L series lens, complete with the signature red band, the striped grips, square condensed typeface, and assortment of graphic embellishments. This final detailing creates an experience that is uniquely Canon.

Canon iPhone app design.

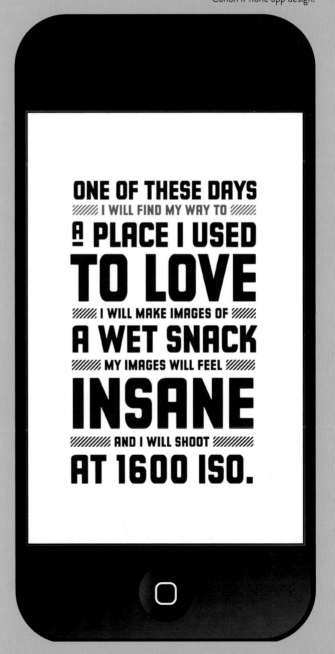

New opportunities and responsibilities

Digital communication has changed the way people interact, connect, and relate to brands. Technology has given customers and users the ability to focus on what they find important, what is relevant to them. They can tune out traditional marketing and advertising. When you visit a website, how often do you pay attention to traditional ad units? You recognize the shape of the ad in your peripheral view and block it out.

That is why brands are trying to be more like people. People like to talk to other people and brands realize they need a deeper connection. They need to have that layer of meaning. Fortunately, this creates new opportunities. Brands need to build relationships that are 24/7, 365 days a year, and talk with, not at, the customer.

Functionality as branding

The most successful brands become nouns or verbs. The brand name comes to represent the entire category of products. Xerox is an example of this. When people "Xerox" a document, they mean photocopy. They may even "Xerox" their document on a Ricoh, or Sharp, or Toshiba.

More often in interactive design, brand is expressed through what a site does—through functionality and behaviors—as much as content, design, and tone. To Google something has come to mean search the Internet for it. It's easy to see why this is so. Google's brand promise of "access to the world's information in one click" is represented through the functionality of the Google search box. It's easy to use. It's fast. It works. Google's brand promise is the functionality of the site.

The strongest Internet brands express their personalities through their functionality and behavior. Look at Facebook's "Like" button. The button contains very little visual design. However, the functionality of this virtual thumbs-up button is synonymous with the brand. It can be found on millions of other websites as other brands desperately try to get you to like them. An Israeli couple even named their kid "Like" after the button—seriously, just Google it. It has been woven into our culture. This button has become a success metric as corporations and businesses look to evaluate the return on investment (ROI) of their social media strategies. There are a lot of other examples branding functionality. Twitter's 140 characters. YouTube's video player. Each of these brands is summed up by what they do. Can you define the next brand by its behavior?

Parkodes were created by Agency Magma as a way to brand the mobile tags used in their World Park Project. Users who scanned these tags during the event in Central Park were rewarded with content related to that specific location in the park. This literal example of functionality as branding helps illustrate how designers can customize functionality, such as QR codes, that may otherwise feel a little lifeless.

PARKODES™

< DESIGNERS AS CODERS >

Designers new to interactive design often ask if they should learn how to code. The simple answer is yes. To be more specific, learn Hypertext Markup Language (HTML) and Cascading Style Sheets (CSS). This book does not try to teach them, but that does not make them any less important.

Ultimately, for a designer, knowing HTML and CSS allows you to understand and control your medium. The lines are blurring between designer and coder, especially with the precision now available to manipulate layout, color and typography through code. Designers will spend countless hours in Photoshop trying different fonts and tweaking little details. However, fonts don't translate perfectly from Photoshop to a browser, so why go back to Photoshop to try a new font? Save yourself some time and play with CSS. If you love your craft, you should be able to understand and engage with every part of it.

You may think that you don't need to learn how to code because you have team members that do it much better. This may be true, but what if you don't always have access to them? Your technology team may be too busy working on current projects to come up with the quick prototype needed to win that next big job. If you can code, you can create the prototype for the pitch, win the job, and leave your development team time to focus on the more difficult stuff.

There are many great resources out there to get you started. Here are a few:

Designing with Web Standards *by Jeffrey Zeldman.*
   New Riders, 2009.
CSS3 for Web Designers *by Dan Cederholm.*
   A Book Apart, 2010.
HTML5 for Web Designers *by Jeremy Keith.*
   A Book Apart, 2010.
www.dontfeartheinternet.com

"Code gives breath to ideas. Knowing how to code is crucial! Knowing how to code well is completely unnecessary."

Pete Denman,
designer, Intel Labs

What Can You Learn from Usability Testing?

Congratulations, you've designed a user experience. But it's been awhile since you've talked to your users. At the beginning of your design project you learned about your client's goals, and then focused on learning all about your users' needs and wants. You took a look at competitors and determined for which platform to design.

Armed with this information, you made strong design choices based on meeting your users' needs. Then you collaborated with your team and your client to design and build a great branded experience.

Hopefully that experience will guide, motivate, and engage your users. But how do you know for sure? How do you validate the assumptions you made in the design process? How do determine how easy it is for the users to learn and use what you've designed? How do you know if you've really met their needs? In other words, after you've designed an experience, how do you continue to put the user at the center of the design process?

You need to get some user feedback on what you've built. One powerful way to continue to include your users, and to incorporate user feedback at the end of the design process, is through usability testing. Usability testing is a technique that is used to evaluate a product by testing it with its intended users. The aim of usability testing is to watch real people use what you've designed to discover any errors they may encounter, how they feel while using it, and to determine ways the experience may be improved.

My Asics

Asics is a Japanese athletic equipment company particularly known for their running shoes that cater to all levels. They understand that serious runners rely on a training plan to analyze their performance and reach their milestones. MyAsics was an online training program they developed for their dedicated runners.

Continued on page 168.

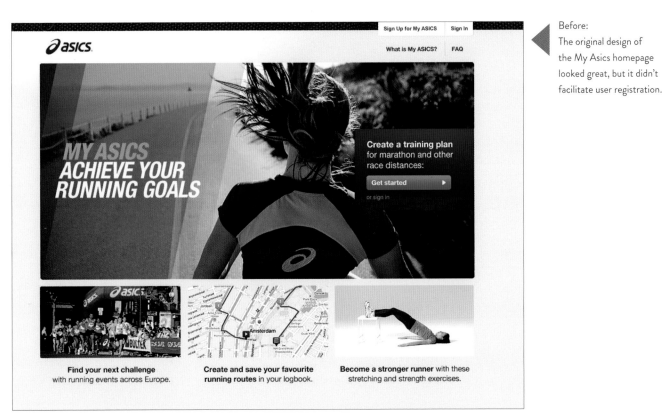

Before:
The original design of the My Asics homepage looked great, but it didn't facilitate user registration.

After:
The new My Asics homepage design wasn't as visually dynamic, but was far more effective at increased user registration.

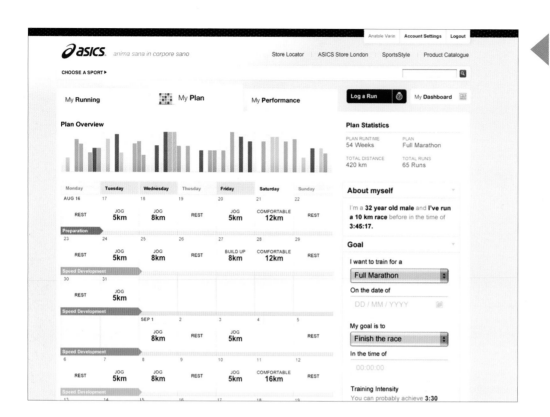

The old My Asics site allowed users to completely customize their workout plan, but it was too intimidating for most users.

The simple questionnaire on the new My Asics homepage helped users start their workout plan in an easy, less intimidating way.

Continued from page 166.

Unfortunately, the company was not getting the number of active users they had expected. In particular, they were having a difficult time getting users to sign up to MyAsics from the homepage. Eighty-seven percent of new visitors left the site from the homepage and only 1.6% actually made it through to the end of the process of creating a new plan. They hired Seabright to give the experience an overhaul and it started with the homepage. Sure, it was beautiful and eye catching, but the design became a barrier. If users decided to actually make a plan on the old site, they were confronted with a confusing list of statistics, settings, and options making it hard for the eye to know where to go. The layout, colors, and grid were visually appealing, but to a user, they made the experience look like a lot of work.

Instead of dramatic imagery and multiple calls to action, Seabright opted for simplicity. A six-question form allowed users to create their running plan with a minimal amount of time and effort. They knew by removing as many barriers as possible users would happily embrace a tool designed for them.

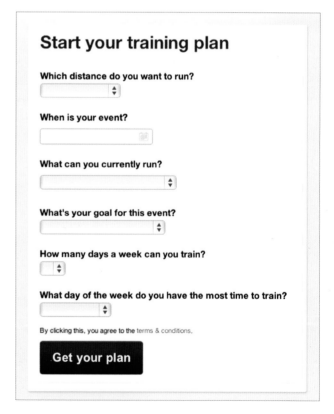

Gino Zahnd, founder at Seabright, talks about how they used usability testing to convince the client of their concept. "Based on some initial concepts, we built a fully functional prototype to test in the browser. In order to get approval from the global manager at Asics, I sent over the following informal email outlining what we wanted to do with the test:

SUMMARY

Seabright will conduct a usability test for the current MyASICS, create a plan and sign up flow, and a prototype of the proposed flow for the same tasks.

PURPOSE

This test is designed to gain insight and answer the following questions:

Qualitative
Which design gives a higher perception of satisfaction?
How much fiddling with the plan happens before the decision to Save & Signup?

Quantitative
Which design yields faster completion times?
Which design yields more plan creation success?
Which design yields more Saves and Signups?

PARTICIPANTS & RESPONSIBILITIES

Six to eight participants will be recruited from our personal network of friends via Facebook, Twitter, and real life in the dirt world. This is the lowest friction approach to find people in our geography who fit the MyASICS audience type.

The tester and moderator is Gino Zahnd. In cases where possible, John Bragg will be the note taker.

Questionnaire
What kind of a runner are you?
Have you ever run a race?
Why do you run?
Do you track your running in any way?
    How? Which services?
Have you ever used a training plan before?
    What was it (online, magazine, coach, etc.)?

EVALUATION PROCEDURE

Location and test facilities
We will have a mobile usability lab, which includes an Apple laptop with built-in camera, and a mouse.

Test session
An hour will be scheduled for each participant, though we expect each session to take less than that.

Test tasks and methodology
There is really only one task flow for this test, so this part is simple.

We will use the following one-line script outline to set up the control scenario:
"You are interested in running the San Francisco Half Marathon on January 1st. You went to Google, search for San Francisco Half Marathon training plan. You saw a link to ASICS and clicked. Here is where you land. Ok, now what?" (or something like that)

Methodology
We will encourage the runner to speak aloud as they go through each design.

We will not lead or help unless asked, or in the case it becomes obvious that the runner needs help.

Apres questions
Which one would you choose?
What's missing?
How much would you pay for a service like this?
How much do you think it costs?
If there were an iPhone or Android app that integrated, would you pay for it?

The manager from ASICS replied with, "OK, go!"

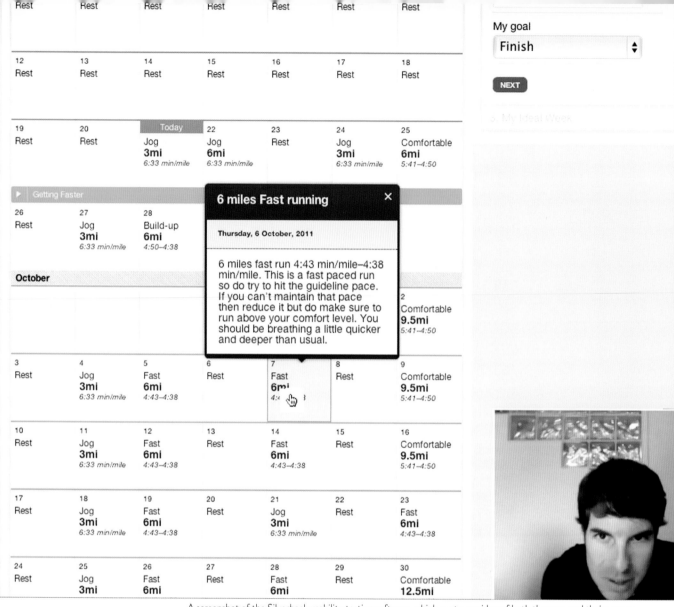

A screenshot of the Silverback usability testing software, which captures video of both the user, and their screen.

Continued from page 169.

"We used Silverback, an inexpensive piece of software for usability testing, to record and analyze our sessions. We followed our proposed plan, and within 5 minutes of the first participant, we knew the new design was going to hit it out of the park."

"After we had conducted five tests, the results were so clear that we cancelled the remaining test sessions. For every metric we tested, the new design shined in every way. Discoverability was far better, time to complete a plan was quicker, and time to save one's plan was much less (in many cases by over 5 minutes!)"

ASICS-UsabilityTests ☆

File Edit View Insert Format Data Tools Help   Last edit was made 34 days ago by ginozahnd

	A	B **MyASICS (starts at the beginning)**	C **Prototype (starts at 10:18)**
1			
2	**Time to complete a tailored plan**	Participant failed to find the 3 steps to tailor the plan. Gino had to show him the 3-step process, and even then, step 1 wasn't clear.	It took 1:10 to reach a fully tailored plan.
3	**Time to Save & Signup**	Participant failed to find the Save button because he failed to see the 3-step wizard. Tried to use the 'Register' link in the navigation bar to save a plan.	It took 2:18 to complete the plan and save it (These two times include him telling us a lot of stuff as he was going through it.)
4			
5			
6	**Notes & Quotes**		
7		Understood there were phases by looking at the whole plan. Liked the phase descriptions.	He'd like a graphic-ish overview of the plan instead of confirmation text. e.g. length of plan, distance, etc. explaining what he's getting into.
8			
9		After being unable to find the Plan Wizard, Gino showed him the wizard. Upon showing him the step-by-step process, he said, "Oh, this is different than the first time I saw this." (It wasn't different.)	*"Compared to the other version, this is meaningful. I can save my plan."* 12:47
10			
11		The slider day picker was confusing. He thought it was a range picker. 5:58	We need to put the EDIT PLAN button in the same screen space as the Edit controls. 13:15
12			
13		Didn't know why entering his age mattered. 7:00	When prompted to log a run, he immediately clicked a date to log the run.. 14:30
14			
15		Saved the plan after 8:00, and after Gino explaining the step-by-step process. 8:00	He assumed there would be a mobile device that would automatically log his runs, and then he'd be able to see them on his calendar in this UI. 15:00
16			
17		Wanted the editor to be the clear thing to do. Didn't even notice the Wizard™. 8:35	*"This is a light year's difference than the previous one in that I have this huge call to action, and I didn't have to figure anything out. All the options were presented to me."* 16:07
18			
19		Thought everything was too text heavy. "I'm not reading any of this."	
20			
21			

Key metrics and important scene markers were noted from the recorded sessions.

"Based on our test results, we were eager to get the new homepage and plan-creation process out into the world. As a litmus test, we decided to launch the newly redesigned screen to a small percentage of visitors to MyASICS via Google ad traffic. The results were awesome. Within the first day, we saw the plan-creation rate go from 1.6 percent to 11.9 percent, an increase of more than 740 percent. We were able to achieve this with less than two weeks of work from concept to launch."

The takeaway is an important one: Beautiful designs do not automatically mean they are good user experiences.

My Asics Website | my.asics.co.uk
Seabright Studios, San Francisco, CA

By sitting back and watching your users learn what you've built, you can gather valuable information. Usability testing is primarily implemented to determine how easy it is to learn and use an experience, but usability testing can also help a designer understand how an application or site is perceived by its users, and what they think of the brand in general.

Usability testing can also be used to start a design project. When a designer is redesigning an existing application or site, it can be a good idea to start by performing some usability tests of the existing experience. This is a great way to meet users and learn about who they are and what they want. The perspective gained by usability testing can be invaluable.

What is usability testing?

There are several different kinds of usability testing—from informal "hallway testing" where a user experience designer recruits and tests their design with five to six random people, to formal usability testing facilitated by a testing professional. But, generally, all usability testing follows the same process—a user representative sits down in front of the application or site to be tested, and she is asked to attempt to perform the tasks it was designed to meet. During testing, a user's interactions with the application or site are recorded, including what they clicked on, how long it took to perform a task, and any errors they made or encountered. The users are encouraged to talk aloud during their explorations, and this running monologue, and their facial expressions are recorded on video. During the test, observers from the design team can watch but are discouraged from talking, interfering with the test, or offering guidance to the user representative. Rather, they are encouraged to sit back silently, watch the test unfold, and take note of areas where the experience confuses or frustrates the users.

FLASHY FIRST-TIME EXPERIENCES CAN ALIENATE REPEAT USERS

by Will Carlin, managing partner, VShift

One of the trickiest aspects of usability design is dealing with both new and repeat users. It is imperative that new users be able to, for example, find the product they are looking for; if yours is a site that many users frequent, you don't want introductory material to slow them down.

We recently had a client who was entranced with a site where the CEO came out from the side of the screen and began talking to you, the user, introducing you to the company and the site. You may have seen these bits of flash that allow you to have just the person walking across the screen instead of the whole video frame. It looked cool, and our client was captivated; he had to have it.

We knew, however, that while it would be very cool once or twice, it soon would turn annoying. With our client's site focused on repeat visitors, we thought it would be a

mistake. But the coolness already had taken hold of our client, and he wouldn't be dissuaded.

So we asked the client to go to this site and do something that was two or three clicks away from the home page and the soon-to-be annoying CEO video. We gave our client ten separate tasks, ostensibly to check out the competitor's usability for those tasks. In reality, while we did want feedback on those ten tasks, we also wanted him to become, in essence, a repeat visitor to the site.

By the end of this little test, he was completely annoyed by the CEO video. The lessons for our client were clear: Always consider your most important user and don't be too wowed by cool; but there also was a lesson for us: Sometimes, the best way to explain usability is to have the client actually, you know, use it.

Usability test plan

The first step in usability testing is to write a test plan. This plan outlines the different tasks that will be tested with the application. These tasks are usually written as simple instructions to your user representatives. For example: "find and play a video" or "register with the site." The test plan also lists the characteristics or traits that are desired in the user-representative testers. These traits can include demographics such as the age, sex, and education of the user, or other information such as their technical expertise or types of interests.

The next step is to recruit user representatives and schedule a time for them to perform the test. The test plan is used to create a questionnaire that recruiters can follow to determine if a potential tester is right for the test. Usability tests often take up to one to two hours to complete, so it is important to make sure the tester has enough time to complete the test.

The third step is to perform the test. After a brief introduction to the purpose of the test by the facilitator, the user is seated in front of the application to be tested. They are then asked to perform the tasks that have been outlined in the test plan one by one. The tester is encouraged to talk aloud as they perform the tasks. The facilitator may answer some of their questions, but will not answer any questions they have about completing the task that is being tested.

It is very important that the tester is not offered any help. The best test results come from watching a user struggle with the application. Their frustration in completing a task indicates places where the user experience is unclear or confusing. Usability software, which records a computer's screen and the user's facial expressions, can be used to record the test for later review.

The final step is to analyze the test results to determine how usable the application is and to propose changes to the design that can improve usability. The facilitator reviews the recordings from the test to determine how easy or difficult it was for a user to perform a task.

Most usability tests measure user responses in four areas:
Efficiency—
    how many steps and how much time was
    required for a user to complete a task.
Accuracy—
    how many mistakes were made
    during the completion of a task.
Recall—
    how much does the user remember
    after they've used the experience.
Emotional Response—
    how does the user feel as they
    attempt to complete the tasks.

Once a facilitator has determined how usable the application is, they use the specific test results to determine what screens or functions the users had difficulty understanding or using. Often, the users will say out loud exactly what the problem is—"I can't find the button" or "I don't understand what that means."

The facilitator suggests changes that can be made to improve usability. Changes can be as simple as rewording a button or as complicated as hiding functionality or information that may clutter the interface and confuse users, behind a tab, or introduce a new nav menu. Proposed changes can be presented as a simple list or as detailed wireframes.

Prioritize the changes from the most important to the least, as well as from the easiest to implement to the most difficult, because the recommended changes will take time and effort. The client will need to determine which changes to implement and which to leave for a future release.

Clients sometimes have difficulty with the prospect of implementing more sweeping changes that may delay the release of the application or site or may increase the budget. It can be necessary to make the case for the proposed changes—especially when making them will affect the schedule and budget. Creating an edited video that shows testers struggling with areas of the application that can be improved with the proposed change can be a powerful tool to make the case.

"By carefully

player (or user)

to understand

the problem in

instead of just

what the user

observing the
one should try
what caused
the first place
designing to
wishes for."

Mattias Ljungström and Marek Plichta,
game designers, Spaces of Play

Psykopaint

Psykopaint is a web-based application that lets you turn your photos into art. The success of a tool like this relies on its ability to make a potentially complex task, like painting, simple and fun. Early usability testing revealed an important discovery: The photo upload screen confused some users, causing them to not complete their paintings.

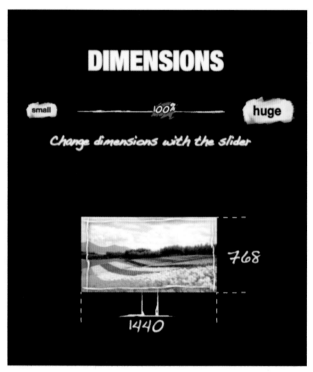

The original photo upload screen overlaid the user's uploaded image on top of the screen size of their monitor. A slider on top allowed users to change the dimensions of the image while the screen size stayed fixed. The Psykosoft team thought this would help visually indicate when the image dimension became larger than your screen.

Users thought the tool was automatically cropping the images to the screen size so they only painted what they saw on screen. As a result, the edges of the photo that extended beyond the screen size would remain unpainted.

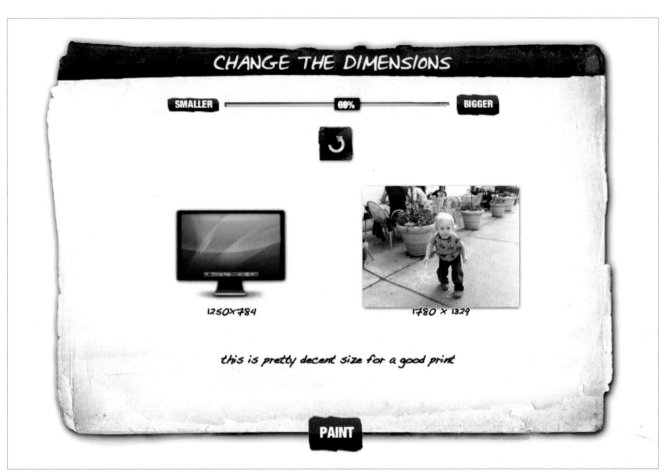

Several tweaks to the photo upload screen improved the experience. The first tweak was to move the screen size and the thumbnail next to each other instead of overlapping. The second tweak changed the actual representation of the computer screen. A real-looking computer screen replaced the solid and dotted white lines, eliminating the confusion that the tool would crop the photo. The final tweak placed separate dimensions underneath the screen display and the photo thumbnail.

Psykopaint Application | psykopaint.com
Pskyosoft, Tours, France

Heuristic Analysis

If it's impossible to perform usability testing because of budgetary or scheduling constraints, a heuristic (or expert) analysis can be performed to gain some insight into how usable an application or site is.

In a heuristic analysis, a user-experience designer stands in as the user representative. The designer reviews the site based on how it complies with recognized usability principles or best practices, also called "heuristics."

There are a variety of lists of heuristics. Jakob Nielsen, called the "king of usability" by *Internet Magazine*, is the author of what is probably the most used list. The heuristics, as published in Nielsen's book *Usability Engineering*, are as follows:

Visibility of system status:
The system should always keep users informed about what is going on, through appropriate feedback within a reasonable time.

Match between system and the real world:
The system should speak the user's language, with words, phrases and concepts familiar to the user, rather than system-oriented terms. Follow real-world conventions, making information appear in a natural and logical order.

User control and freedom:
Users often choose system functions by mistake and will need a clearly marked "emergency exit" to leave the unwanted state without having to go through an extended dialogue. Support undo and redo.

Consistency and standards:
Users should not have to wonder whether different words, situations, or actions mean the same thing. Follow platform conventions.

Error prevention:
Even better than good error messages is a careful design that prevents a problem from occurring in the first place. It either eliminates error-prone conditions or checks for them and presents users with a confirmation option before they commit to the action.

Recognition rather than recall:
Minimize the user's memory load by making objects, actions, and options visible. The user should not have to remember information from one part of the dialogue to another. Instructions for use of the system should be visible or easily retrievable whenever appropriate.

Flexibility and efficiency of use:
Accelerators—unseen by the novice user—may often speed up the interaction for the expert user such that the system can cater to both inexperienced and experienced users. Allow users to tailor frequent actions.

Aesthetic and minimalist design:
Dialogues should not contain information that is irrelevant or rarely needed. Every extra unit of information in a dialogue competes with the relevant units of information and diminishes their relative visibility.

Help users recognize, diagnose, and recover from errors:
Error messages should be expressed in plain language (no codes), precisely indicate the problem, and constructively suggest a solution.

Help and documentation:
Even though it is better if the system can be used without documentation, it may be necessary to provide help and documentation. Any such information should be easy to search, focused on the user's task, list concrete steps to be carried out, and not be too large.

ADDITIONAL USABILITY TECHNIQUES

Eye tracking
Eye tracking is the process of measuring where a user is looking at a screen, by measuring their eye position and eye movement. Traditional usability evaluation techniques provide information about where a user clicks. Eye tracking offers the ability to understand where a user is focused in between clicking. Eye tracking data in usability evaluations is used to understand which features are eye-catching, which are confusing, and which ones are ignored altogether. Eye tracking requires expensive technical equipment and so is infrequently used for usability evaluations.

A/B testing
A/B testing is a technique primarily used by marketing firms, where two versions of the same experience, such as a banner ad, email, landing page, or shopping carts are presented to different users. User interaction is then tracked to determine which version, A or B, results in more user clicks or a higher percentage of sales. The "winner" is then used for the final ad, email, landing page, or shopping cart. A/B testing isn't used to understand why one version is more usable or successful than the other.

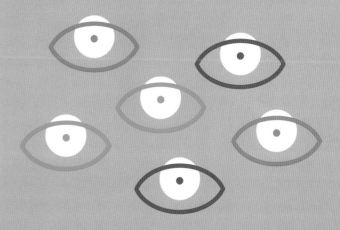

USABILITY TESTING ON THE CHEAP

By Gino Zahnd, founder, Seabright Studios Ltd.

Usability test labs range from expensive corporate labs with one-way mirrors, viewing rooms, wireless A/V equipment, and multiple-person teams, to mobile one-person guerrilla operations. We've found that a small mobile setup provides every bit of the value a lab does, and many times removes the awkwardness people feel when they are placed in a formal lab room with a one-way mirror. After all, if the people testing your software aren't comfortable in their environment, are you getting reliable results? Here are a few ways to get huge value with a minimal budget.

TEAMS

We nearly always have two people run usability tests. One person administers the tests, and one takes notes. Two people aren't necessary, but can reduce the time to synthesize results and provide additional insights. If you're working on a shoestring budget, one tester can suffice, assuming some basic equipment is available.

TOOLS

For testing desktop products, we've distilled our "test lab" down to one piece of equipment: a laptop. Seabright is primarily a Mac shop, so all our laptops have a built-in camera. For the same reasons, we don't favor test lab environments, we also favor the built-in camera; it's less invasive and less intimidating than an external camera. People forget it's there and focus on the product.

SALE!

Illustration by Samantha Katz and Andy Pratt

One of our favorite pieces of software for usability testing is Silverback. It's dirt simple to use, and it records screen activity, the participant's face and voice, the tester's voice. It also allows you to mark key points on the video, and you can control recording sessions with the Apple remote. Everything is easily exported to a picture-in-picture Quicktime movie, which shows the screen and the participant's face. It's great to have that shareable video when you discover the usability pattern that helps you prove that pesky executive team wrong. . .

Silverback doesn't work well for observers in real time, but for us it isn't an issue because we prefer no-lab environments and do the sharing and observation to a wider audience with the recorded video after the tests are finished. Doing things this way tends to be a better use of everyone's time as well.

For people/companies that use PCs, Morae is a less elegant, but more in-depth set of tools for usability testing, observation, and analysis. It's also significantly more expensive than other tools, and I would not consider their software bundle price "on the cheap" when compared to Silverback. That said, the Morae components can be purchased separately, which can help cut costs.

I can't discuss software tools without also mentioning paper prototypes. Sitting down one on one with folks who might use your product, and asking the right questions, can provide equally valuable revelations to help your product succeed. Testing concepts on paper doesn't require technology and oftentimes fosters better discussion than an on-screen experience can. People aren't intimidated by paper.

TOOLS DO NOT A CRAFTSMAN MAKE

Lastly, none of this is meant to imply that anyone can buy software and magically be a usability expert. Like any area of expertise, there are many methodologies and techniques to learn before one can become proficient. There are lots of ways to elicit responses from participants, and to structure and execute test plans. There's a spectrum of prototype and product fidelity on which to conduct tests. All of these hinge on, of course, knowing what to test. Sometimes, a larger budget is required to get results, but in our experience, huge value and product improvements can be derived from testing with narrowly scoped, highly focused plans, and a $49 piece of software. Any company can afford that.

Three useful links:
http://silverbackapp.com/
http://www.techsmith.com/morae.html
http://www.alistapart.com/articles/paperprototyping/

13

If You Build It, They Won't Always Come —
Marketing the Experience

You can design a delightful and useful experience that meets your users' needs in unique ways, and it may not succeed. If your customers don't know about what you've designed, if they don't realize how it can help them, and if they don't connect to it emotionally, they will not visit your site or use your app.

Successful projects require more than just creating something useful, usable, and desirable that meets user and client needs. You must market your experience to your customers, let them know that it exists, explain how it helps them, and ultimately foster an emotional connection between your users and what you've designed. The role of marketing is to generate conversations between your brand (the product you've designed) and your target audience (your users) to convey the ideas, concepts, and values of why they should use your product.

ALO Drinks

ALO, makers of the delicious drink of the same name, launched a new campaign aimed at separating themselves from the competitive aloe vera juice market. Their marketing position was simple: Play a more active role in the health of their consumers. Understanding that their target audience already lead a healthy lifestyle through exercise, yoga, and dietary choices, they realized they could not just sell the drink. They had to sell and market an experience.

Continued on page 186.

Drink.

Listen.

Share.

New Leaf (ALO Exposed) ALOtone
ALOdrink.com
ALOtones™ : Free music in every bottle

www.YourFBpage.com

SocialMedia

Write something...

ALO Drink Presents:
New Leaf
(ALO Exposed)
ALOtone™
m.ALOdrink.com

ALOtones bring Goodness From Inside Out™. Enjoy free music mixed for each flavor, inside every ALO Drink.

Share

alo

®

Aloe Vera

+

alo
EXPOSED™
ORIGINAL + HONEY

Free music!

ALO bottle design.

Continued from page 184.

Their tagline, "Goodness from Inside Out," represents their commitment to using only natural ingredients to deliver the best possible product. Working with Agency Magma in NYC, ALO looked to add another ingredient to the bottle. It wouldn't alter the flavor, texture or color, but it would change the drinking experience. The latest ingredient they added was music.

The music, termed ALOtones, are specifically designed for each flavor. QR or Quick Response Codes found on the product labels allow customers to scan, listen, download, and share. Customers that don't have a smart phone can text message shortcodes.

ALOtones is a powerful, emotional ingredient that provides an effective marketing hook. By integrating digital into a traditional product, a new experience was created that was greater than anything the product could offer by itself.

ALO Drinks | alodrink.com
Agency Magma, New York, NY

The trade booth encouraged people to take a moment, sit down, and taste each flavor by listening to the music.

1. Scan   2. Download   3. Listen   4. Share

ALOtones marketing experience.

RATIONAL VS. EMOTIONAL

by Michael Ferrare, founder, Agency Magma

Do people buy your brand based on rational or emotional decisions? Look at the socks below. The low-priced tube sock on the left provides the same function as the high-priced designer sock on the right. Both products are made of cloth, come in multiple colors, and are likely to wear out at the same speed. A consumer simply looking for a functional pair of socks will rationally choose sock A. However, a consumer looking for a sock that fits their personality will likely choose the higher-priced designer sock. Sock B charges a premium because it comes with the additional "emotional" layer of being "designed."

Do you want your brand to be seen as the rational choice or the brand that fits an identity and reached consumers on an emotional level? What does the market need? Neither approach is right or wrong, however, brand consistency is crucial.

Recommended reading:

Duct Tape Marketing: The World's Most Practical Small Business Marketing Guide *by John Jantsch. Thomas Nelson, Inc., 2011.*

Marketing in the Age of Google, *by Vanessa Fox. John Wiley & Sons, Incorporated, 2010.*

OPTION A
$2.00

OPTION B
$16.00

Illustration by Michael Ferrare

How the web has changed marketing

For the past twenty years, marketing, like the music and publishing industries, has undergone some radical changes. The web has enabled whole new forms of marketing and new ways of doing business.

With the introduction of online advertisement in the form of banner ads, paid search results, and Google AdWords, marketers are able to track the efficacy of their campaigns in whole new ways. Prior to the web, the most common way of judging the effectiveness of an ad campaign was through surveys or focus groups, where customers were asked if they remembered an ad and what they thought of it. In the age of the web, it is possible to see exactly where a customer saw an ad, if they clicked on it, and what percentage of those customers who clicked actually purchased the product.

Marketers have come to rely on this data to determine how successful a campaign is, to make changes to that campaign to make it more effective, and to learn about customer habits so as to better reach them with future campaigns. This data has revolutionized the marketing landscape.

Web searches, in particular, have created a whole new channel for marketers. According to *Marketing in the Age of Google*, Americans search the web 29 million times per minute. Google supports the bulk of its business through sponsored search results and AdWords. Companies pay to appear at the top of a user's search results for specific keywords.

Search engine optimization, or SEO, is the process of improving a site's position in unpaid (aka natural) search results. As more and more websites are launched and more users resort to search engines to find what they're looking for, SEO has become a powerful marketing tool. SEO is vital in improving the ability of users to find your website.

For interactive designers, it is important to understand the basics of search engine optimization. But this can be tricky. Because search engines constantly change their algorithms—the way they catalog and rank websites—the most effective methods for optimizing SEO change. In general, search engines are concerned with aboutness and importance. Aboutness is what the page is about and how close it is to what a user is searching for. Importance, or rank, indicates how significant the value of the page is to the user. This combination is used to determine what goes into a search result and the order in which those items are displayed. It's important to take into account how search engines determine aboutness and rank when designing a webpage.

An important part of marketing is positioning—letting your users know how your product is different from your competitors. Marketing is about identifying this differentiation and communicating it to potential customers.

Good marketing doesn't just let people know that you exist or that you have a new site or app. Good marketing connects a brand with a customer often, and with a consistent message or value proposition. This consistent transfer of values over time resonates and will make a lasting impression with your customers.

Equally important in marketing is determining how and where to communicate the message to customers. Much like what you've already learned about user-centered design, it is important to understand who the customers are. Knowing details about the customer helps determine what kind of language to use to clearly communicate to them, and where in their daily lives they will be most receptive to hearing a message about the product.

Modern marketing relies on collected data about consumers, such as demographics—age, income level, education, etc.—their spending habits, where they spend their time, etc., to paint a picture of a potential customer, and then make decisions about how to communicate to them, and where to reach them. This "how and where" is often called media.

For example, marketing to doctors is very different than marketing to patients. For one thing, there are far fewer doctors than there are patients. Doctors speak with a specialized language. They are often interested in different aspects of a product than patients would be, and reaching doctors requires different methods of communication, or media, than reaching patients. Patients can be reached through radio and television. Reaching doctors may require advertising in trade magazines or direct contact via email or phone calls.

Traditional　　　　**Influence Swell**
                              |

Digital

When traditional and digital media campaigns are aligned, marketers often see a lift in the performance and effectiveness of their campaigns. There is in essence a swell. In order for this swell to happen, interactive and marketing departments need to work together. Sounds simple, but departments are often siloed, missing opportunities to have more of an impact.

WHAT IS MARKETING?

Marketing is the interface between a business and the world. Marketing clearly communicates the who, what, when, where, and why of a product to potential customers. If a business can understand these details, then it will understand its "brand."

Marketing provides a business with a vocabulary and tools to communicate how its product is different from its competitors' and the product's value to potential customers. All in the name of encouraging an emotional connection.

OUTDOOR MEDIA

PRINT

MOBILE

GAMES

RADIO

PRESS

DVR

TV

INTERNET

By understanding your core consumers, you can choose the shapes, mediums, and touchpoints that are most relevant and therefore most effective.

Illustration by William Ranwell

Earning loyalty

One way marketers categorize media is if it's paid or earned. The difference is simple. Paid media is purchased by the marketers, and hence is guaranteed. An example of paid media would be a print ad in a magazine where the publisher charges $6,000 a month for a single-page advertisement that (according to data) is guaranteed to reach a certain amount of people, within a specific demographic. In other words, you pay for what you get.

Earned media is not guaranteed. Instead, it's what can be called "people media" or "social marketing." It's buzz. Earned media are stories that people pass along directly to their friends. Today, you can see if your marketing ideas are gaining traction by tracking or researching what people are doing with them. Are customers sharing your website? Is there a reason for them to do so?

Social networks have created a lot of new opportunities for marketers. Platforms such as Facebook, Twitter, and YouTube make it easy for customers to share marketing messages. Marketers and clients are beginning to understand the value of being able to connect directly to their audience through social channels. And more online activities are becoming social experiences, such as social shopping, social viewing, and social collaboration.

The power of peer recommendation mixed with the reach of our social networks makes ideas spread faster than ever before. But social media needs to be used appropriately by the brand. Customers need to believe in a brand or product in order for them to want to connect, share, and have a dialogue about it. Do you really want to hear what your bank has to say, or the local funeral home up the street?

When you market your experience, it is important to include hooks that encourage your customers to share your campaigns. Clients that choose to use social marketing need to be fully committed. There is nothing worse than a stagnant feed or dormant blog. Earned media means earning customer loyalty, and that requires a commitment to provide them with something special or useful.

The ultimate goal of marketing is brand loyalty. When the marketing message is honest and clearly communicates the true values and benefits of what you've designed, customers will come to trust your brand and will become more loyal. They may even choose your next product versus a competitor's simply because of the brand loyalty you have built up over time.

THE ADVANTAGES OF TRADE-OFFS
by Will Carlin, managing partner, VShift

Marketing often is about trade-offs. You want to reach as many people as possible, but you have a limited budget. You want your ad to say everything about you, but you have limited space. You want people to remember you, but you have only a few attempts to get in front of them.

Trade-offs are not always compromises, however, and sometimes they even force focus. A small budget requires detailed audience understanding: who are they, where do they go, and what do they do? Once you know that and your budget, you can figure out exactly how many attempts you have to catch them.

And then, of course, design kicks in. Whether you are reaching them via email, a banner ad, a video ad, or even a real-life mailer or television ad, you have to get across a lot in a little. Oh, and let's make it memorable, okay?

That's why design and marketing go hand in hand; you want the right message, the right design, and the right format going to the right people at the right time in the right place. You need to plan it well and have them all in mind to get all those "rights" to work together.

Watch, Learn, and Adapt

By now you've learned how powerful it can be to incorporate users in your design process—learning who they are, and taking their wants into account. Designing and building an application or site that meets the real needs of real people is not only a useful design philosophy, it can be very fulfilling as well. You may have made your users' lives easier, their jobs more pleasant. You may have provided them with more free time by reducing the amount of time they would have spent performing a specific task, or you may even have given them something new and exciting that they weren't even aware that they wanted.

The extra time you spent getting to know your users was time well spent, and all the ways that you incorporated real people in your design process—from your initial user research to usability testing your finished designs—was invaluable in making strong design choices. But how do you know that what you've designed will stand the test of time?

The way people use tools and applications changes over time. Their understanding and acceptance of a tool will change the more they use it. They will even find new ways to use it and new places where it can be used.

When automobiles were first introduced, they were seen as a luxurious oddity. They were expensive, complicated, and required special training and knowledge to use. Roads were designed for horses. Gasoline was not readily available. People were afraid of traveling fast. Early cars looked more like what they were called at the time— horseless carriages. But look at cars now. They are sleek, fast, and equipped with GPS systems, satellite radios, antilock brake technologies, and power steering. The design of the car has evolved over the decades.

There were many steps in that evolution—it took an innovator like Henry Ford to mass produce automobiles and make them affordable and an infrastructure of roads and gas stations to make cars accessible to a broader user base. But soon they stopped being an oddity and became a useful tool, and after that they became a desirable design object.

Spirits App

Spirits is an action-puzzle game for the iPad, iPhone, and Mac created by Spaces of Play. Users try to move their spirits to a destination by one of four different actions: blowing, digging tunnels, growing bridges of leaves, or blocking wind. The concept is simple, but the execution is really beautiful.

Continued on page 196.

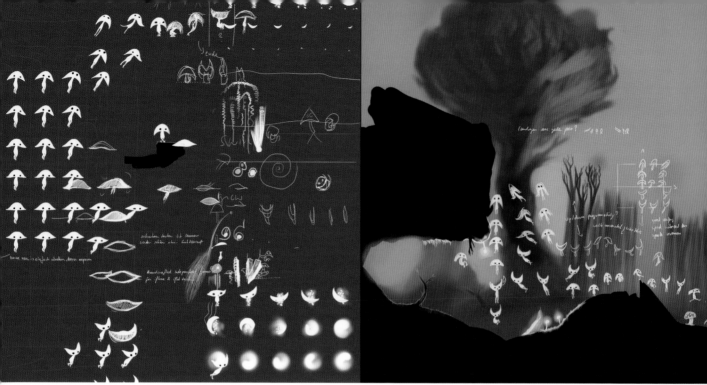

Sketches of the spirits reacting to wind.

Continued from page 194.

After the initial launch of the game, the team decided to make a couple of important tweaks based on watching their users. One of them dealt with how a core game mechanic, wind, was implemented. In the initial release of the game, spirits would jump in the air and get carried away by the wind only once they reached a steep edge. Users did not understand this.

Instead, users would make a blowing action, wrongly assuming that spirits could be blown into the air from flat ground. In future releases, the team decided to allow spirits to be blown into the air from flat ground. Not only does this match what users expected, but it also allows users to speed up the pace of the game since they no longer have to wait for spirits to get to an edge. Wind does not simply transport the spirits from point A to point B; it brings them to life. They dance and float, creating an atmosphere that is both relaxing and dreamy, much like the art itself.

Spirits can be found in the iTunes store.

Spirits App
Spaces of Play, Berlin, Germany

Millions of users started to use and want cars. As people found more uses for the automobile—from using trucks to deliver goods, to busses that transported multiple people over long distances—the evolution of the automobile sped up. Numerous changes—both large and small—in technology and design created the cars that we know and love today.

Interactive systems like websites and applications evolved in the same way. To enter input into the first computers, you inserted paper cards punched with little holes into a mechanical device that translated those holes into ones and zeros. Now, we use keyboards, computer mice, touch screens, and voice recognition software. The first computers used printers similar to old typewriters to display information. Now, computers display that information through 3D computer graphics on screens that display millions of colors, with audio, and even vibrations. The first computers filled entire rooms with vacuum tubes. Now, we carry powerful computers thousands of times more powerful than those early models in our pockets.

Computers have come a long way in just half a century of design evolution. But what about what you've designed? A website or application?

Facebook launched as a website where college students could connect with other college students, communicate with each other, and share photos. Today, Facebook is used by close to a billion people. New features are constantly introduced, tested out, and updated based on how the growing user community interacts with the site. Some of the features Facebook introduced over its short life include the ability to play games, record and share videos, instant message other users, and comment on other users' status updates. And now Facebook is no longer just a website, it's a platform that can be accessed by users on their mobile devices, their computers, or even from other websites.

Facebook constantly watches what its users do. And it watches its competitors as well to see what new features they offer. By continuing to incorporate user feedback into the process, watching how its users interact with the site and competing sites, continuing to learn about the new things that they want, and adapting to meet those needs, Facebook has come a long way in less than a decade. And Facebook continues to evolve. To stay successful, it needs to stay relevant to its users.

In fact, all successful interactive products continue to put their users at the center of the design process after the initial design has been completed. How do they incorporate user-centered design practices after they've launched? By continuing to watch what their users and competitors do, by learning from these new user behaviors about new user needs and wants, and by adapting to meet those needs in the simplest, easiest to use, most elegant way possible.

"The most
time for a
be involved
is all the time
launch is
most critica

mportant
designer to
in a product
But after
perhaps the
time."

Khoi Vinh, cofounder, Mixel,
and blogger, Subtraction.com

Phase in functionality

The first step in watching, learning, and adapting to meet new user needs and goals is to make sure that there is enough empty space in what you've designed for your users to imagine the new things they might like your product to do for them. This is a bit of a tricky concept. You want to launch a product with a core feature set that feels complete and offers users with an easy-to-understand story of what needs it can meet, but you don't want to tell such a detailed story that they can't imagine new ways to use what you've designed. New functionality is then phased in over time, as the design team learns how your product is being used and what new stories its users want to tell.

For example, when Flickr launched, its core feature set was simple—uploading photos and sharing them with other users so they could comment on the photos. Flickr started as a simple, public photo-sharing network. What they left out was more important than what they included. The idea that was different with Flickr was that a user's photos could be shared publicly to other users they didn't know who simply followed them. There was little emphasis on inviting family members or friends to view a set of photos the way you would on Flickr's competitor sites. They didn't offer photo printing or the ability to make photo albums. They didn't lock users into the story of the traditional way photos had been shared. Flickr left plenty of open space in their initial product for their users to imagine all kinds of new ways to use the site.

And Flickr's users did. They used Flickr to share photos with random strangers, to give other users photography advice, and to create social connections over shared photographic interests with users who they had never met in real life. It wasn't long before Flickr's users met each other in real life through ad-hoc meet ups to go on photography outings.

And as Flickr's users imagined new ways to use the site, and new ways to think of digital photography, Flickr phased in new functionality to meet their changing needs. Flickr introduced the ability to create photo sets that included other users' photos, so users could create tours of their favorite photos on Flickr. They introduced the ability to tag and comment on a part of a photo, so users could give specific photographic advice on composition or technique. They even introduced the ability for users to upload short videos, though they called them moving photographs to maintain emphasis on Flickr's core story.

Flickr adapted to evolving user needs. But they couldn't have done so if they had locked users into a story that was so specific that there was no room to imagine new ways that Flickr could be used. Flickr launched with a simple feature set that told a simple but open-ended story—a story that would still engage and compel its users, but one that left open possibilities. And then Flickr phased in new functionality as users figured out the new ways they wanted to use the site.

In other words: Don't launch with it all. Leave room to adapt.

'Sometimes, the simplest tweaks can yield huge results... There is always room for improvement. Always be on the lookout for simple and inexpensive things you can do to provide a better user experience."

Jon Phillips,
website and UX designer

Watch what your users do

But how do you learn about new user needs and wants? How do you learn about the new stories your users want to tell using your product?

Start by watching what they do. How do they currently use what you've designed? What sections of the site do they visit the most? Which sections, the least? What kinds of content do they look at or listen to? Are there sections of the site where they get hung up? Are there any forms, shopping carts, or processes where they seem to be having difficulty?

There are a variety of ways you can watch what your users are doing. The methods already discussed in this book—from focus groups to surveys, from ethnographic research to usability evaluations—are all still applicable and are powerful tools to learn what users are doing. But once a site has launched, you have another powerful tool at your disposal—metrics.

One of the more powerful aspects of the web is the ability to track what individual users are doing. These user metrics allow companies to understand a huge amount about their users—what they click on, what pages they visit, how long they stay on a particular page, and what pages of the site they leave—are all metrics that can be tracked. Metrics won't tell you what your users think or want, but they can point you in the right direction. If you notice from the metrics that users are abandoning a shopping cart at a particular step, then it's probably a good idea to perform a heuristic evaluation, or usability test of that step, to see where users may be stumbling.

After you've launched your site, start with metrics and then add in focus groups, surveys, ethnographic research, and even usability evaluations to learn more.

Watch what your competitors do

The other powerful way to understand how your users' wants and needs may be evolving is to watch your competitors to see what new features they are offering. This will give you insight into how user perception is shifting, and what users may want or not want.

When the social network Google+, a competitor to Facebook, launched it included a feature that allowed users to group their contacts into circles. Circles enabled users to send updates to a subset of their connections rather than to all of them. The feature produced a lot of buzz. It was blogged about, and the resulting publicity helped Google+ gain millions of users in months. Circles were even talked about as the feature that could make Google+ a potential "Facebook killer"—until Facebook added their own user groups shortly after Google+ gained so much publicity.

Facebook watched its competitor, learned about the new wants of its user base, and adapted to meet those wants.

Enhance the existing experience to meet new user needs

But Facebook didn't just copy Google+'s Circles. They created their own way to group contacts. Facebook's groups were not as powerful as Google+'s Circles, but they were simpler to use, easier to set up, and still met user needs. Facebook evolved based on watching its competitor and continues to evolve to meet user wants and needs. The company watches its users and competitors closely to help determine what those needs and wants are, but it never copies.

Watching competitors to gain understanding of evolving user behaviors is about learning. It isn't about copying a design or feature. It's never a good idea to just copy a competitor. It's important to always enhance or customize the new feature to better meet your particular users' needs. Once you have learned about the new features your users want through watching them, and your competitors, it is important to continue to think about your client's business goals, the success metrics that tell you if you've met these goals, the device you are designing for, the brand, how you will continue to guide, motivate and engage the users, and all the other pieces of information you have gathered during the design process.

New features should never feel bolted on, added as an afterthought, or as a response to competitive pressures. Any new features you phase in over time must enhance the overall experience of what you've designed. They should fit elegantly into the already existing story, adding to the utility and pleasure offered by the experience to your users.

THE DESIGN PROCESS NEVER TRULY ENDS

by Damien Newman, CEO, Central

The design process never truly ends. From the initial stages of observing, learning, and generating insights from which to design, to crafting prototypes, developing interactions for experiences, it is a continuous participatory loop. Design is at least one part organizational transformation. All projects are collaborative and demand support and participation from many sources inside an organization to the actual constituents of the designed solution. So after creating the solution, there's much more to be done to make it succeed in its launch. The Helsinki Design Lab in Finland calls it "design stewardship" where "designers must be involved, providing expertise and feedback to identify, test, and deliver durable solutions." This is something we practice in our process in working with clients. In particular with one client, Urban Re:Vision, we've been working with them for several years developing and refining their products and strategies as we help them relaunch and grow. These products we've been working on range from an ultimate guide to planning and running a Re:Vision workshop, to a book with 1,000 photographs, and a workshop showing the nonprofit's vision in action.

Initially, Re:Vision, a nonprofit organization dedicated to helping communities redesign themselves with a whole-systems approach, came to us three years ago to help with designing a workshop. The seventy-nine-person event was for the San Francisco mayor's office to redesign the city's civic center area downtown.

Inside the project room for Urban Re:Vision including the research and inspiration for developing a toolkit for workshops.

Uncertainty / Patterns / Insights

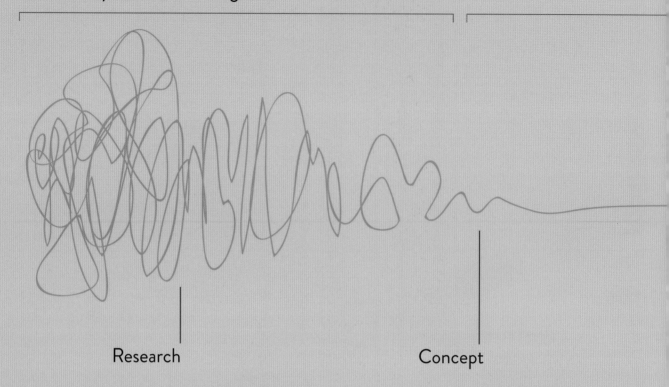

Research

Concept

From there, having a first-hand experience in designing and delivering one of their services, we began to work on articulating their core offerings and developing products for them to sell. One of the things we've worked on for the last year is developing a comprehensive guide to running a Re:Vision workshop. This involves bringing together different community constituents—along with architects, developers, and city officials to look at the site for redesign—and allowing the people within these communities to design through a human-centered, whole-systems approach. Think Buckminster Fuller Design Science + Biomimicry Institute, Biomimetic solutions. We've been researching and learning everything we can about transforming people, helping people co-

create in workshops, and how to break down Re:Vision's framework for design into actionable exercises for people to do. It's like having a team in a workshop imagine all the future, delayed, good or unnoticed failures that might be happening in a particular area of a city site. Another exercise includes creating a time-lapsed story of an ideal moment in a city block, integrating all the ideas and insights a group has created.

Clarity / Focus

Design

We've been creating a full-version prototype to run in the real world to see how it performs. We worked with Re:Vision to select a partner to test the workshop guide, who immediately responded enthusiastically and suggested we do so with them in Haiti, to assist with the rebuilding efforts there. So we're going to actually co-lead the workshop with Re:Vision and their partner, in the field where it can make the most impact, to learn how we can adapt and improve our initial prototype to be more successful.

For us, we're able to shorten the design process (as shown in the design squiggle) where the flat end of the squiggle is focused in refining a single concept, and take the earlier steps to deliver something, and measure it in the field—where it is in the hands of the actual people using it. Because we're on hand, seeing the way people actually use something, we're able to advise on what things we should or could do to make adjustments. D-Rev, a local Bay-area product design firm, focused on social innovation, aptly illustrates the design process as going a step beyond delivery, into scaling and measurement—two vital parts of the process to ensure continual success. It's where you take a hand in being there when all that you researched, conceived of, and imagined would happen, does or doesn't do so exactly as you thought.

Illustration by Damien Newman

We hope that you have found this book to be a useful introduction to user-experience design (UXD) and user-centered design (UCD) practices. We've attempted to explore the history of user-experience design from its roots (the study of efficiency)—in human—computer interaction—to today, where modern designers apply a variety of tools. These tools range from ethnographic research techniques to usability testing to design successful user experiences. Designers use these techniques to focus on the needs and wants of the people who will use what they design.

We've made a strong case that designing to meet the real needs of real people is a powerful and fulfilling design philosophy that results in a focused design process and, ultimately, a better, more useful, and more successful design.

We have walked you through the UCD process—from learning what your client wants, to defining success metrics, to learning about your competitors and your users. We've also explored the opportunities and constraints of designing for different platforms. We've highlighted the importance of branding the experience, as well as guiding, motivating, and engaging your users, testing and marketing your design, and continuing to evolve it after it's launched.

Along the way, we've presented useful tips and techniques to empower you to apply UCD to your own design process. And we've shown you examples of today's designers who apply those processes on a regular basis to design remarkable, enjoyable, successful, and useful products that are so successful precisely because they meet the needs of their users so well.

Window to the World

Toyota Motor Europe (TMW) and the Copenhagen Institute of Interaction Design (CIID) joined forces to conceptualize a new way for car passengers to wile away the often-tedious hours of travel.

Continued on page 210.

Brainstorming the possibilities at Toyota Motor Europe

Synthesizing the research findings

Continued from page 208.

Toyota's "Window to the World" turns the average car window into a futuristic smart window, so passengers can explore, play, and learn about the landscape they are driving through. This interactive, transparent canvas not only allows users to finger paint, but also displays information (such as name and distance) of passing objects. Users can also pinch and zoom in for greater detail.

Projects like this change our expectations of interactive, both where it belongs and what it can do. However, some things stay the same. Context, as always, is important. In this project, for example, how might this smart window function differently depending on the traveling environment, be it a highway, country back roads, or a busy city street?

See the concept video. Search for "Toyota Window to the World" on YouTube.com.

Toyota/CIID Case Study: Window to the World
Copenhagen Institute of Interaction Design (CIID) &
Toyota Motor Europe, Kansei Design Team

User-experience design as a profession has exploded in recent years. Following the introduction of the web, and the Mosaic and Netscape browsers in the mid-90s, the need for experienced and talented interactive designers has increased almost exponentially. Computers have gone from being the domain of highly trained technical experts, and early adopter hobbyists, to becoming a useful and ubiquitous tool for everyone from grandmothers to grade-school kids. As they transition from the desktop, to the laptop, to the pocket, to our television screens and appliances, and beyond, they will become more ubiquitous, more useful, more a part of our everyday lives. They will become more essential and more trusted.

More and more, we use computers to meet a variety of daily needs and wants—from paying bills to finding entertainment, from deciding where to eat to staying in touch with our friends and family. Computers give us driving directions and the news. They provide us with useful information about where we are on the planet and empower us to express ourselves in new and exciting ways. They engage and entertain us. And we expect them to do all this smoothly, easily, and with minimal effort. We expect our computers to be as easy to learn and use as our automobiles, televisions, and phones. In fact, we expect them to be seamlessly and invisibly integrated with our cars, TVs, phones, and other traditional technologies, to enhance how those technologies meet our needs and wants.

In many ways, computers are becoming invisible, and will continue to do so. When we reach into our pockets and pull out our cell phones to find a place to eat, or message a friend on Facebook, we are no longer consciously aware that we are interacting with a user experience that has been specifically designed for our computer or device screen—but we are. Interactive design is everywhere—anywhere there is a screen that we can interact with, and even some objects without screens such as our credit cards or personal data gathering devices like Nike Fit or Fitbit. Interactive design is found in our computers, laptops, phones, televisions, tablet computers, cars, the seat backs in airplanes, ATMs, cameras, appliances, watches, even in chips embedded in our credit cards.

In fifty years, computers that would have filled office parks have shrunk to fit on our wrists. And the computing power of these devices we wear on our wrists is exponentially more powerful than their ancient relatives. It's been just over fifteen years since the introduction of the World Wide Web. Since then, there has been an explosion of websites, web users, and different ways users connect to and access the increasing functionality and power of the web. More people today access the web on their mobile devices than on traditional computers. And that's just the start. What will the next innovation be? Ten years ago, there was no YouTube, no Facebook, no iPods, no Android phones, no tablet computers. What will we see in the next ten years?

Interactive design has changed radically in just twenty years. It continues to do so, becoming more varied and complex with each passing year.

More screens on new devices

Networked and connected computers are everywhere, from our desktops to our pockets. And every day new devices hit the market with different form factors, different-sized screens and sensors, offering different sets of functions. Technologies such as augmented reality allow designers to layer data over the real world. GPS lets a device know where it is at all times. And technologies such as RFID, Bluetooth, and wireless allow devices to talk to each other and gather data from each other.

Where will your next go-to screen be? Your watch? Glasses? You car windshield? We have no idea. But whatever the form factor, or feature set, a user experience designer will need to design the software that makes it useful and delightful.

Trends

In the late 90s, no one foresaw the draw and power of social networking. Nobody looked into their digital crystal balls and saw the power of the mobile web or smartphones. And certainly no one at the time could have imagined a teenager making a Facebook update on their Android-powered phone, after having checked in with Foursquare to become mayor of their local coffee shop, texting their friends, and then killing some time waiting for them by playing a quick game of Angry Birds.

It would be foolish of us to pretend that we could look ahead from our vantage point today and divine the next big advances in the interactive world. But we can present some of the trends that we see emerging and make some guesses about them. In other words, we're going to do it anyway.

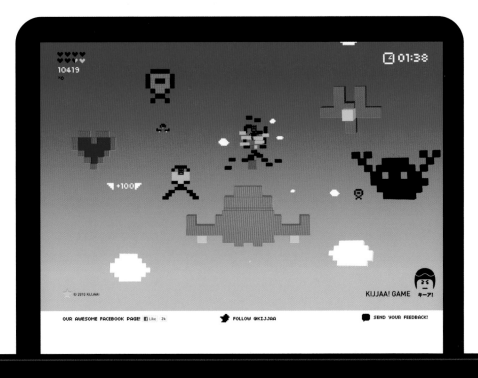

The iPhone app is the controller
for this browser based game.

Kijja!

Kijjaa! is an 8-bit style desktop web game that turns an iPhone or iPod Touch into the game's controller. After downloading the app, users key in the code found on the website, and they're ready to battle. The game makes full use of the devices' built in accelerometer and gyroscope, which results in a truly responsive experience.

Grisha Sorokin, Kijjaa! founder, got the idea one night as he was sitting in his office, thinking about the future of iPhone gaming. With the phone in his hand, he began to twist and turn it, and Kijjaa! was born. According to Grisha, he expects to see more integrated experiences like this in the future. As ownership of mobile devices swells, advances in technology create a perfect environment for innovation.

Download this app. Search for Kijjaa! in the iTunes store.

Kijjaa! Website and Mobile App | www.kijjaa.com
Grisha Sorokin, Moscow, Russia

Here are some trends we see in interactive design that we think are going to be important to tomorrow's user-experience designers:

New ways to interact

And as these devices become more sophisticated, we are given new and better ways to interact with them, from multitouch screens to voice commands. Deciding the right ways that users can interact with a device will depend on how and when that device is used and what it is used for. Will users want keypads to enter text? Will they be in situations where they can talk clearly enough for voice recognition to operate properly? And how will they be given feedback, and what kinds of ways will users need to be guided when using these nontraditional data entry methods?

Research and testing with users will be invaluable to determining the answers to these questions.

More data collected, more data everywhere

Our devices will learn more about us. Sensors such as GPS are already integrated into our phones and devices. New sensors that collect a variety of personal data from the number of footsteps we take in a day, to our heart rate, blood pressure, and even how well we sleep, will be increasingly ubiquitous. We will expect access to this data when and where we need it. And we will expect it to be safe and private.

With each new data source comes new complexity—complexity that will be simplified and made useful by a user-experience designer.

Experience ecosystems

And as we acquire more and more devices, and those devices gather more and more data about us, we will expect them to work together. We will want access to the personal data gathered on our watch from our last exercise session—maximum heart rate and number of calories burned—on our mobile device to help us make decisions such as where and what to eat.

Or we may want to control our televisions with our cell phones or play games on our tablet computers using our wristwatches as game controllers. Devices will need to work seamlessly with each other, passing data, displaying information, and interacting. And these intradevice experiences—these experience ecosystems—will need to be designed, more likely than not, by a user-experience designer.

THINK RESPONSIVE

It is becoming increasingly difficult to design for the plethora of screen resolutions available on the market. It is even harder to future-proof your design for new resolutions. Despite these challenges, many clients want websites that look great on a variety of screens: They want them mobile, tablet, and desktop ready. What to do? It is not practical to design for every possible screen resolution.

One of the growing options to tackle this fragmentation is to make the site responsive. Responsive sites are designed with a flexible grid so they can adjust to the viewer's browser width. So a site on a small mobile screen displays the same information as a larger desktop screen, however the layout has been dynamically adjusted. This does not mean to simply shrink or enlarge the experience, but rather redistribute, alter, and remove content, navigation, and user-interface elements to make the best experience possible.

It sounds great. But in order to design this way, you must change the way you work. You can no longer think in terms of pixels. Your designs will not be pixel perfect. Yikes! Instead, think in terms of percentages. The elements you're designing get a percentage value so they can be resized.

Besides changing the way you work, you may also need to change the way you review designs with your client. Instead of making flat comps for each screen resolution, make prototypes.

There are still hurdles that need to be explored, like the best way to efficiently use images or how to handle ad units. Despite the challenges, momentum for this approach is growing. New solutions are always being developed to tackle complex sites with difficult functionality and demanding business rules, making it a viable alternative to the fixed width design.

Learn more about responsive design from the creator: Responsive Web Design *by Ethan Marcotte. A Book Apart, 2011.*

THE FUTURE OF BRANDING

by Randy J. Hunt, creative director at Etsy

The future of branding lives in a place where boundaries overlap and edges are fuzzy. It's a place where online and offline have merged, where products and brands are inseparable.

To look into the future, it may benefit us to look at where we've come from and where we are right now. Where we've been is a place where designers operated as storytellers, wrapping businesses and ideas in consistent narratives communicated with visual wit, novelty, and efficiency. Many designers today have come to a new place: they are conceiving, designing, and branding products of their own.

Now, we're on the verge of something special. It's a place where designers are creating products and building brands simultaneously. The product becomes the main expression of the brand and the brand itself can be looked at as a product. This is especially true when we look at web products.

In this world, the product itself is the expression of the brand. The response to a swipe, a unique gesture, or a notification sound can all establish and reinforce the qualities of a brand.

This extends beyond simply being "branded," but rather experienced. You see when we swipe, tilt, and share, you are participating in the creation, propagation, or revealing of the brand experience.

As interaction (or experience) designers, we have a unique opportunity. We're able to craft those experiences. In fact, I'd not call it an opportunity. I'd call it a responsibility.

Social

And these new devices will be at their most useful to us when they connect us to the people that we care about. Social networking isn't new. We've been creating social networks and connecting to our friends for hundreds of thousands of years. But now, with the advent of digital social networks we are able to make and maintain connections with people from our past such as from school or college, our professional lives, and even people we never meet in real life with whom we share interests. The type and strength of connections become more important when we can share personal information passively such as our location or the content we consume, like the books we read.

Social networking offers users powerful utility, but when privacy and user comfort isn't taken into account, those same social networks can be frightening or overwhelming. Designing an experience that incorporates social networking from a user-centered perspective where a user's needs and concerns are taken into account, mitigates the prospect of alienating your customers.

Customized, personalized, and individual

Ultimately, the most successful new experiences will provide us with what we want, when we want it. They will anticipate our needs and provide us with content, information, news, connections, and functionality without us actively asking for it. User experiences in the future will learn who we are and what we want, and then they will give it to us. They will offer suggestions of new content that may interest us based on our consumption habits. They will know who our primary contacts are and what we like to share with them. These new applications will provide us with a unique and individualized experience, tailored to us specifically.

User-centered design

The future of interactive design is rich. More and more experiences will need to be designed. Our expectations will continue to become more sophisticated. New technologies will provide us with new sources of data. We will expect more, want more, and need more from the experiences with which we interact. But it doesn't really matter what new wonders the future brings. New devices will be released. We will be given new ways to interact with them. They will know more about us. They will talk to each other, sharing data. They will continue to connect us to the people we care about. And ultimately they will give us what we want, when we want it. If they are designed to do so.

Future interactive experiences will be successful only if they continue to meet our needs and wants, in simple, easy-to-learn, easy-to-use ways. In other words, if we designers continue to put real people at the center of our design process, if we work to understand who they are and what they want, then design applications will meet those needs in useful and exciting ways.

"The best is invisible of the way you live

interface
t gets out
and lets
your life."

Amber Case,
cofounder, Geoloqi.com

RESOURCES

The following list includes the books, websites, and people mentioned in the book as well as a few others we suggest you check out.

Websites to visit:

5by5.tv - @5by5
Broadcasts for designers, developers, entrepreneurs, geeks, and nerds.

alistapart.com - @alistapart
For people who make websites.

boxesandarrows.com - @boxesandarrows
The design behind the design.

**dontfeartheinternet.com -
@jessicahische & @strangenative**
Basic HTML & CSS for non-web designers.

fastcodesign.com - @fastcodesign
Welcome to Fast Company's Co.Design, where business and design collide.

gamification.org - @gamification
The Gamification Wiki for Game Mechanics & Gamification Research.

geeksugar.com - @geeksugar
From simple how-to instructions, to tips, cool websites, tech toys, and news.

lynda.com - @lyndadotcom
Helping you learn, master, and apply digital tools and techniques.

mashable.com - @mashable
The largest independent news source covering web culture, social media and tech.

measuringusability.com - @msrusability
Usability & Statistics: If people do it we measure it.

methodandcraft.com - @methodandcraft
Method & Craft explores the creative mind and the beauty within each pixel.

netmagazine.com - @netmag
The world's bestselling magazine for web designers and developers since 1994.

offscreenmag.com - @offscreenmag
A new, collectible magazine about the human side of interfaces

patterns.ideo.com - @ideo
We are a global design consultancy. We create impact through design.

psfk.com - @psfk
Your go-to source for new ideas and inspiration.

rockpaperink.com - @rockpaperink
A place for designers to come together to share their opinions, creations, and passion for the field.

sectio 508.gov
Resources for understanding and implementing Section 508

silverbackapp.com - @silverbackkapp
Usability testing software for designers and developers.

smashingmagazine.com - @smashingmag
An online magazine for professional web designers and developers.

techcrunch.com - @techcrunch
Breaking technology news and opinions

techsmith.com - @techsmith
Screen capture and recording software for individual and professional use

ted.com - @tednews
All the news from #TED: TEDTalks, TED Conferences, the TED Prize and more.

tuaw.com - @tuaw
The unofficial Apple weblog.

useit.com
Usable information technology

uxmag.com - @uxmag
Defining and informing the complex field of user experience (UX) through frequent publication of high-quality articles for experts and newcomers alike.

uxmovement.com - @uxmovement
A progressive user experience/interface blog designed to make the web a better place.

uxpond.com - @uxpond
A search engine dedicated to user experience blogs, journals, discussion, events, UI patterns, and tools.

uxurls.com - @uxurls
User-experience aggregator

w3.org
The World Wide Web Consortium (W3C) is an international community where member organizations, a full-time staff, and the public work together to develop web standards.

Books to check out:

100 Things Every Designer Needs To Know About People
by Susan Weinschenk. New Riders, 2011.

Content Strategy for the Web, 2nd Edition by Kristina Halvorson and Melissa Rach. New Riders, 2012.

CSS3 for Web Designers by Dan Cederholm.
A Book Apart, 2010

Designing for Interaction: Creating Innovative Applications and Devices (2nd Edition)
by Dan Saffer. New Riders, 2009

Designing with Agile by Anders Ramsay.
Rosenfeld Media, 2012.

Designing with Web Standards
by Jeffrey Zeldman. New Riders, 2009

Don't Make Me Think by Steve Krug. New Riders, 2005

Duct Tape Marketing: The World's Most Practical Small Business Marketing Guide by John Jantsch.
Nelson, Thomas, Inc., 2011.

Handbook of Usability Testing: How to Plan, Design,
and Conduct Effective Tests, 2nd Edition
by Jeffrey Rubin and Dana Chisnell.
John, Wiley & Sons, Incorporated, 2008
HTML5 for Web Designers
by Jeremy Keith. A Book Apart, 2010
Learning Web Design
by Jennifer Niederst Robbins, O'Reilly. 2012
Marketing in the Age of Google by Vanessa Fox.
John, Wiley & Sons, Incorporated, 2010.
Mobile First by Luke Wroblewski. A Book Apart, 2011
Ordering Disorder: Grid Principles for Web Design
by Khoi Vinh. New Riders, 2010
Responsive Web Design by Ethan Marcotte.
A Book Apart, 2011
Sketching User Experiences: Getting the
Design Right and the Right Design
by Bill Buxton. Elsevier Science, 2007.
Tapworthy: Designing Great iPhone Apps
by Josh Clark. O'Reilley Media, 2010
The App & Mobile Case Study Book
by Rob Ford and Julius Wiedemann. Taschen, 2011
The Design of Everyday Things
by Donald A. Norman. Basic Books, 2002.
The Elements of Content Strategy
by Erin Kissane. A Book Apart, 2011
The Elements of User Experience:
User-Centered Design for the Web and Beyond
by Jesse James Garrett. New Riders, 2010.
The Graphic Designer's Electronic-Media Manual:
How to Apply Visual Design Principles to Engage
*Users on Desktop, Tablet, and Mobile Website*s
by Jason Tselentis. Rockport Publishers, 2012
The Internet Case Study Book
by Rob Ford and Julius Wiedemann. Taschen, 2010
The Web Content Strategist's Bible
by Richard Sheffield. CreateSpace, 2009

25 People to follow on Twitter:

Aaron Koblin - @aaronkoblin
Artist, nerd, Google Data Arts Team ringmaster
Amber Case - @caseorganic
Cyborg anthropologist studying the interaction
between humans and technology. UX Designer.
TED Speaker. Cofounder of Geoloqi.com
Anders Ramsay - @andersramsay
Designer, maker, entrepreneur
Claudia Bernett - @claudybee
Digital artist/designer & principal at Collective Assembly
Dan Saffer - @odannyboy
Author of *Designing for Interaction and*
Designing Gestural Interfaces.

Dana Chisnell - @danachis
Principal Researcher at UsabilityWorks
Jared M. Spool - @jmspool
Just a dude who thinks a lot about creating
great user experiences.
Jeffrey Zeldman - @zeldman
Author, *Designing With Web Standards.* Founder,
Happy Cog™ design studios, A List Apart.
Co-founder, An Event Apart, The Big Web Show.
Publisher, A Book Apart.
Jennifer Bove - @jenniferbove
Interaction designer, principal at Kicker Studio.
Jennifer Robbins - @jenville
Interaction and visual designer, O'Reilly author,
mom, interviewer of rock stars.
Jon Phillips - @jophillips
Maker of fine things that live on the interwebs.
UX designer, musician, entrepreneur.
Josh Clark - @globalmoxie
Designer, developer, mobile maven, 11th strongest
man in Maine, author of *Tapworthy*, creator of
Couch to 5K, rascal.
Kel Smith - @kelsmith
Creative technologist striving for a greater good.
Khoi Vinh - @khoi
Cofounder of Mixel.cc, blogger at Subtraction.com,
former design director at NYTimes.com.
Kimberly Bartkowski - @kimmiikat
Digital creative director @arnoldnyc.
Kristina Halvorson - @halvorson
CEO and founder, Brain Traffic
Linda Holliday - @lmholiday
Angel Investor, entrepreneur, starting new
premium digital publishing company
Liz Danzico - @bobulate
Part designer, part educator, and part editor
Luke Wroblewski - @lukew
Digital product design & strategy guy in Silicon Valley,
CA. Known for Mobile First, Bagcheck, Web Form
Design, & more...
Matt Jones - @moleitau
Vapid proclamations across all of spacetime.
Nick Myers - @nickmyer5
Managing director of visual design + branding @cooper.
Randy Hunt - @randyjhunt
Creative director at Etsy among other tales of triumph,
victory, and love.
Seth Godin - @thisissethsblog
Founder of Squidoo.com, author, blogger.
Susan Weinschenk - @thebrainlady
Psychologist, UX, author
Whitney Hess - @whitneyhess
Independent user-experience strategist and
management consultant.

CONTRIBUTORS

AGENCY MAGMA
USA
agencymagma.com

ALL THINGS MEDIA
USA
allthingsmedia.com

ANDERS RAMSAY
USA
andersramsay.com

CARBONE SMOLAN AGENCY
USA
carbonesmolan.com

CENTRAL
USA
centralstory.com

CLOCKWORK ACTIVE MEDIA SYSTEMS
USA
clockwork.net

COPENHAGEN INSTITUTE OF INTERACTION DESIGN
DENMARK
ciid.dk

DINIS MEIER AND SAMUEL BAUER
Zurich University of the Arts
SWITZERLAND
zhdk.ch

DREAMSOCKET
USA
dreamsocket.com

ETSY INC.
USA
etsy.com

FUNNY GARBAGE
USA
funnygarbage.com

GEOLOQI
USA
geoloqi.com

GESTURE THEORY
USA
gesturetheory.com

GOOGLE
Worldwide
Google.com

HAPPY COG
USA
happycog.com

JON PHILLIPS
Canada
jonphillips.com

KHOI VIHN
USA
subtraction.com

KICKER STUDIO
USA
kickerstudio.com

KIJJAA!
Russia
kijjaa.com

LUDLOW KINGSLEY
USA
ludlowkingsley.com

METHOD INC.
USA
method.com

NEW YORK CITY DEPARTMENT OF HEALTH AND MENTAL HYGIENE
USA
nyc.gov/health

POP
USA
pop.us

PRICETAG
USA, Ecuador
pricetaghq.com

PSYKOSOFT
France
psykosoft.net

READABILITY LLC
USA
readability.com

SEABRIGHT STUDIOS LTD.
USA
seabrightstudios.com

SECOND STORY INTERACTIVE STUDIOS
USA
secondstory.com

SEMI-LINEAR
USA
http://semi-linear.com/

SEVNTHSIN
USA
sevnthsin.com

SPACES OF PLAY
Germany
spacesofplay.com

TAG CREATIVE
USA
tagcreativestudio.com

USABILITYWORKS
USA
usabilityworks.net

VSHIFT
USA
www.vshift.com

WELIKESMALL
USA
welikesmall.com

ABOUT THE AUTHORS:

Andy Pratt has over twelve years of experience creating award-winning interactive media. He has delivered vision and strategy to some of the largest brands in the world, including the Smithsonian Institution, Sesame Workshop, Cartoon Network, Noggin, The-N, Wenner Media, Lego, and Turner Broadcasting. Andy is also co-founder of Pricetaghq.com, a custom quoting tool for interactive businesses. He is an adjunct professor at the School of Visual Arts, where he teaches about interactive media in the MFA program, "Designer as Entrepreneur." Andy is also a creative director at Funny Garbage, an interactive agency in New York City.
www.andypratt.net
@andyprattdesign

Jason Nunes has used a story-based, user-centered design process for more than fifteen years to help create innovative, intuitive, and fun experiences for software, the web, the mobile web, apps, and devices such as set-top boxes. Jason has managed international projects, led tight-knit teams, and worked as a solo consultant for a variety of clients across multiple verticals including media and entertainment, finance, telecommunication, healthcare, and technology.

Some of his clients include ABC News, the BBC, Citibank, CNN, Coca-Cola, Eidos Entertainment, ESPN, ILM Commercial Productions, McGraw-Hill Higher Education, MetLife, Monster, MTV, Nokia, NPR, Orange, Reuters, the Smithsonian Natural History Museum, Teen Nick, and *Vogue*.
www.jasonnunes.com
@monkeyprime

ACKNOWLEDGMENTS

We would like to thank all of our contributors, colleagues, and friends for their, ideas, time, and support. In particular, we would like to thank Sarah Coombs for her guidance. We would also like to call out a few others who have gone above and beyond: Michael Ferrare, Kimberly Bartkowski, Suzanne Nienaber, Dan Willig, Kristin Ellington, Jennifer Bove, Scott Gursky, William Ranwell, Junko Bridston, Damien Newman, Tony Pratt, Julia Turner, Lisa Armand, John Carlin, and Funny Garbage.

We would also like to thank the team at Rockport Publishers who put it all together with their hard work and attention to detail.